HUMAN VALUES IN EDUCATION

[XX]

THE FOUNDATIONS OF WALDORF EDUCATION

RUDOLF STEINER

HUMAN VALUES
IN EDUCATION

10 Lectures in Arnheim, Holland
July 17–24, 1924

Ⓔ Anthroposophic Press
2004

Published by Anthroposophic Press
SteinerBooks
400 Main Street
Great Barrington, MA 01230
www.steinerbooks.org

Translated from Rudolf Steiner's *Der pädagogische Wert der Menschenerkenntnis und der Kulturwert der Pädagogik*, (GA 310), Rudolf Steiner Verlag, 1989. Previous English edition by Rudolf Steiner Press, London, 1971; translated by Vera Compton-Burnett, revised. Published by permission from *Rudolf Steiner Nachlassverwaltung*, Dornach, Switzerland.

Revised edition copyright by Anthroposophic Press © 2004

This edition was made possible through the generous support of
THE WALDORF CURRICULUM FUND

Library of Congress Cataloging-in-Publication Data

Steiner, Rudolf, 1861–1925.
  [Pädagogische Wert der Menschenerkenntnis und der Kulturwert der Pädagogik. English]
  Human values in education : 10 lectures, Arnheim, Holland, July 17–24, 1924 / Rudolf Steiner.— Rev. ed.
    p. cm. — (The foundations of Waldorf education ; 20)
  Includes bibliographical references and index.
  ISBN 0-88010-544-5
  1. Waldorf method of education. 2. Anthroposophy. I. Title. II. Series.

LB1029.W34S7362517 2004
371.39—dc22

                                    2004009171

Contents

Introduction

Christopher Bamford

Although each of Rudolf Steiner's courses of lectures on what has come to be known as Waldorf education has its own special quality and value, certain seminal courses shine out with a unique light. *Human Values in Education* (originally entitled "The pedagogical value of knowledge of the human being and the cultural value of pedagogy") is certainly one of these. It was held in July1924, which was the last glorious year of Steiner's active life—he died in 1925. The context was a summer teachers' conference, set in an unusual part of Holland among wooded hills. Participants were united not only by lectures, but also by meals, excursions, and almost continuous discussion and conversation. Thus they created what Günther Wachsmuth described as an "a splendid mood of intensive community." Two months later, Steiner would give his last lecture, the so-called "final address" (September 28, 1924).

It is not only sentiment that makes Steiner's last active year remarkable. The year began with the founding of the General Anthroposophical Society with Steiner at its head (January 1, 1924). This was more than simply an important event: it represented the flowering and culmination of Steiner's entire life and work. What followed in the next nine months, as it were, cast the seeds of this fruition forth into the world. As he united his own karma with that of the Society, Steiner had said that he did not know how the spiritual world would regard his action. He warned members that his sources of inspiration might dry up. The spiritual world might not be willing to cooperate. Fortunately, this was not the case. Far from abandoning Steiner, the spiritual world heaped grace upon grace upon him and he, out of his own inner forces, responded with a newfound simplicity, contemporaneity, and directness. It was as if he had fulfilled his obligations to his historical, spiritual lineages—theosophical, occult, and so on—and could now speak directly from the heart in the common language of human experience. This is what gives *Human Values in Education* its freshness as an overview of the unique qualities of Waldorf education— what makes it special.

Waldorf education is, of course, based on knowledge of the human being acquired on the basis of anthroposophy or spiritual science, which means that it starts from precise, phenomenological observation of the whole being as body, soul, and spirit. As such, there is nothing "theoretical" about it. Education today, like so much else, suffers from a split between theory and practice or actuality. Most educational philosophies are theoretical and divorced from life. They experiment with children, because they are no longer able to approach them with their hearts and souls. Education therefore does not deal with the reality that lives between teachers and students. For Steiner, this is symptomatic of "the fundamental evil behind all the frequent social disturbances in today' society": "the failure to acknowledge others and the lack of interest people should show for one another." It is a sad fact, but mostly we pass each other by without ever knowing or recognizing each other. To overcome this abyss, teachers must learn to love again. Without love, it is possible neither to gain the knowledge necessary to teach, nor to teach.

From the point of view of love, children are entrusted to us for their education. They are a sacred trust we receive. Our job as parents and teachers is not to develop them toward some abstract ideal, but to welcome them and midwife their entry into earthly life. Steiner is quite clear: "When we deal with young children, we are faced with beings who have not yet begun physical existence; they have brought down soul and spirit from pre-earthly worlds and plunged into the physical bodies provided by parents and ancestors." When we observe a child what we see is soul and spirit seeking to take hold of life. A divine being who previously lived in the spiritual world has come to live among us. Those who greet this being "have a sense of standing before an altar." But the usual function of the altar is reversed. Rather than holding our offerings, this altar is for the gods to reveal to us the divine, spiritual-cosmic laws by which the world was created. Every child becomes a mystery and poses a question. Not how to educate him or her to some preconceived end, but rather how to nurture what the gods have sent to earth. Waldorf education is a pedagogy based on the reverence and love that necessarily follow from this kind of thinking. In this light, the teacher is not so much an instructor, as an artist, whose calling is more priestly than profane.

There is nothing programmatic about this. It is not a question of applying principles, but of responding to *reality*, that is, to the individual children, each of which brings to earth certain inherent characteristics that we must learn to intuit and nurture. Meeting the children (besides the parents) are those we call teachers, who are also individual beings. Between the two, individual teachers and students, the relationship that is education germinates, grows, and, if successful, flowers. To become a teacher in this context is more like becoming a gardener. One must know one's plants, as well as the soil and climate, and on the basis of this knowledge, one's "green thumb," become an improvising, loving artist.

Observing the unfolding of children in this way, we notice first that the process of entering earthly life occurs through progressive, developmental stages. Steiner explains that these begin before birth, continue throughout life, and constitute an interconnected whole, so that what happens earlier has a consequence later. He also emphasizes the importance of recognizing that they are not fixed. Children's development today is not the same as it was five hundred, a thousand, or four thousand years ago. Again, it is necessary to be absolutely realistic and responsive to what is before one. And what is before is always an individual. In that individual, a whole world is revealed—"not just a human world, but also a divine spiritual world manifested on earth." Each child represents a world and an aspect of the world; and is an opportunity for teachers to enrich their understanding with a new perspective. Every class is thus a kaleidoscope of perspectives—of evolving beings. Learning to work with these, a teacher becomes an artist, aware that what he or she does has significance for world evolution.

The nine lectures that make up *Human Values in Education* fill out this picture of child and teacher engaged in the complex dance of body, soul, and spirit that we call "education." Throughout, Steiner weaves seamlessly and lightly between micro- and macro-perspectives. In the second lecture, he considers the process if incarnation in terms of a whole human life, taking the German poets Goethe and Schiller as his examples. (These would have been familiar to his audience; had he been talking in America today, he might well have drawn on Emerson and Thoreau.) From this, he turns to the miraculous events of learning to walk, speak, and think—and from these to the three stages of childhood (from birth to the change of teeth, from the change of teeth to puberty, from puberty to adulthood.) At every opportunity, he moves from the detail to the whole, from the specific to the universal. Above all, Steiner practices what he preaches: these lecture are *alive*.

The volume falls into three movements. We begin with lectures that weave around the development of the child into a full human being of body, soul, and spirit. This allows us to understand the practical pedagogic aspects of the education. It is followed by a couple of profound, insight-filled lectures discussing more the more social-spiritual aspects of education as practiced in Waldorf schools: teachers' conferences and parent-teacher meetings. Finally, in his last lectures, Steiner turns to questions arising under the general rubric of the temperaments as these relate, once again, to body, soul, and spirit.

No such lecture cycle is ever complete in an encyclopedic way, but each nevertheless covers "the basics" in its own way. Any lecture by Rudolf Steiner also has its own incomparable value. Yet this sequence is truly extraordinary and incomparable in a different way, both because it is the last that Steiner gave on education and because, in his last months, Steiner was graced with a remarkable clarity and penetration that allowed him to address old topics (as well as new) with uncanny spiritual luminosity, precision, and sheer humanity. If anyone is looking for the "last word" on Waldorf education, this is perhaps it— in more ways than one.

1 | The Need for Understanding the Human Being

July 17, 1924

$\mathcal{F}$or quite a few years now, education has been an area of civilized cultural activity that we nurture in the anthroposophic movement. And it will become obvious in these lectures that it is specifically in this area that we can look back with some satisfaction at what we have done. Our schools have existed for only a few years, so I cannot really speak of accomplishment, but we can speak of the beginning of something that, even outside the anthroposophic movement, has already left an impression on groups interested in the spiritual life of culture today. In reviewing our educational activity, it gives me real joy to speak again on this closely related theme—particularly here in Holland, where many years ago I had the opportunity to lecture on subjects related to anthroposophic spiritual science.

Anthroposophic education and teaching is based on knowledge of the human being, which is acquired only on the basis of spiritual science; it works from our knowledge of the whole human being as body, soul, and spirit. Initially, such a statement may be seem obvious. It will be said that, of course, the whole person must be considered when it comes to education as an art—that spirit should not be neglected in favor of the physical, nor should the physical be neglected in favor of spirit. The situation will soon be obvious, however, once we see the practical results that arise from any area of human activity that is based on spiritual science.

In The Hague, here in the Netherlands, a small school—a daughter, so to speak, of our Waldorf school in Stuttgart—was established on the basis of an anthroposophic knowledge of the human being. I think that anyone who becomes aware of such a school, whether from merely hearing about its practices or in a more intimate way, finds that its methods arise from an anthroposophic basis and are essentially different from the typical school today. This is because, wherever we look today, we find a gap between what people think or theorize and what they actually do in practice; in our present civilization, theory and practice have become widely separated. Although it may sound paradoxical, perhaps this separation can be seen above all in the most practical of all occupations in life—in the world of business and economy. Here, all sorts of things are learned theoretically. For example, people think through the details of administration in economic affairs. They form intentions, but those intentions cannot be performed, because no matter how carefully they are thought through, they do not meet the reality of life.

I would like clarify this so we can understand each other. Let's say a man wants to set up a business. He writes up a business plan, considering everything related to this business and organizing it according to his intentions. Then he acts on his theories and abstract thoughts, but here they must deal with reality. Certain things are done; invented ideas are put into practice, but the thinking does not fit real life. In fact, something is carried over into real life that does not correspond to reality. A business conducted in this way may continue for awhile, and those who start such businesses may consider themselves to be very practical. Those who go into business and never learn anything beyond the customary practices generally consider themselves to be "practical" people.

Today we can hear truly practical people speak of such theorists, who enter the business life and introduce their theories with a heavy hand. If enough capital is available, they may be able to continue for awhile, but with time the business fails or may be absorbed into another, more established business. Usually when this happens, very little attention is given to how much genuine, vital effort was wasted, how many lives ruined, and how many people were injured or hindered in life. It has happened only because something has been theorized—thought out by "practical" people. In such cases, however, their practicality has not come through understanding but through the intellect. They introduced something into reality without considering the actual situation.

Few people notice, but this sort of thing has become rampant in today's society. Now the only area where such matters are understood—where it is recognized that such a procedure does not work—is in the application of mechanical engineering. When a decision is made to build a bridge, it is essential to use the knowledge of mechanics to ensure that the bridge will hold up to what is required of it; otherwise, the first train to cross it will plunge into the water. Such things have happened, and even today we see the results of defective mechanical construction. In general, however, this is the only area of practical life where it can be said unequivocally whether or not the conditions of reality were foreseen.

If we consider the practice of medicine, we see immediately that it is not so obvious whether or not the conditions of reality have been properly considered. Here, too, the procedure is the same; something is theorized and then applied as a method of healing. It is indeed difficult to perceive when there is in fact a cure, when it is a person's destiny to die, or when one has simply been "cured to death." The bridge collapses because of defects in construction; but it is not so easy to see what causes a sick person to get worse, to be cured, or to die.

Likewise, in the realm of education, it is not always possible to see whether growing children are being educated according to their needs or according to the fanciful methods of experimental psychology. In the latter case, a child is examined externally, and then one asks about the child's memory, intellectual capacities, ability to form judgments, and so on. Educational goals are frequently formed in this way. But how are they carried into life? They sit firmly in the head; that is where they are. Teachers know *in their heads* that a child must be taught arithmetic one way, geography another, and so on, and then the intentions are to be put into practice. Teachers must consider all that they have learned and recall that, according to the precepts of scientific educational methods, they must proceed in a particular way. Then, when faced with putting their knowledge into practice, they recall various theoretical principles and apply them in an external way. Those who have a gift for observing such things can experience how teachers—even when they have thoroughly mastered educational theories and can recite everything they had to learn for examinations or in practical classroom teaching—may nevertheless remain completely separate from life when faced with the children they must teach. What happened to such teachers is the same thing we are forced to observe with sad hearts, daily and hourly: the fact that people pass one another by in life; that people have no sense for really getting to know one another.

This situation is common and the fundamental evil behind all the frequent social disturbances in today's society. It is the failure to acknowledge others and the lack of interest that people should show toward one another. In everyday life, we must accept this state of affairs; it is the destiny of modern humanity at the present time. But such aloofness reaches its apex when the teachers of children and young people stand separate and apart from their students, while employing conventional scientific methods in a completely external way.

When a bridge collapses, we can see that the laws of mechanics have been applied incorrectly, but wrong educational methods are not so obvious. People today are comfortable only when it comes to mechanical thinking, which can always determine whether things have been thought out rightly or wrongly, and which has led to the most brilliant achievements in modern civilization. This is clear from the fact that humanity today has confidence only in mechanical thinking. It is an indication that people no longer have a natural talent for approaching children themselves when mechanical thinking is carried into education—when, for example, children are asked to write out disconnected words and then repeat them quickly, so that the teacher can record their powers of assimilation. We experiment with children because we are no longer able to approach their hearts and souls.

Having said all this, it might seem as though we are merely inclined to criticize and reprove with an air of superiority. It is, of course, always easier to criticize than to build constructively. As a matter of fact, however, what I have said does not come from such an inclination or desire; it comes from observing life in a direct way. And such observation of life must arise from something that is usually completely absent from today's knowledge. What kind of person does it take to pursue a calling based, for example, on knowledge of the human being? *One must be objective*. This can be heard everywhere today, in every hole and corner. Of course, we must be objective, but the question has to do with whether or not such objectivity is based on a lack of attention to what is essential in any given situation.

In general, people have the idea that love is the most subjective thing there is in life, and that it would be impossible for anyone to love and be objective at the same time. Consequently, when people speak of knowledge today, love is never mentioned in a serious way. True, when young people apply themselves to acquiring knowledge, it is considered appropriate to encourage them to do so with love, but this is usually done while the whole presentation of knowledge is very unlikely to develop love in anyone. In any case, the essence of love— giving oneself to the world and its phenomena—is certainly not considered to be knowledge. Nevertheless, for real life, *love is the greatest power of knowledge*. And without this love, it is impossible to acquire knowledge of the human being, which forms the basis of any true art of education.

Let us try to picture this love, and see how it can work in the special sphere of an education based on knowledge of the human being, as drawn from spiritual science, or anthroposophy.

Children are entrusted to us for their education. If our thinking in regard to education is based on spiritual science, we do not view a child as something to be developed toward some human ideal of society, or some such thing; a human ideal can be completely abstract. Such a human ideal has already assumed as many forms as there are political parties, societies, and other interests. Human ideals change according to one's adherence to liberalism, conservatism, or some other program, and thus children gradually taken in some particular direction to become whatever is considered proper. This is carried to extremes in Russia today. In general, however, this is more or less the way people think today, though perhaps somewhat less radically.

This is not the place to start for teachers who want to educate on the basis of spiritual science. They do not idolize their own opinions. An abstract image of the human being, toward which children are to be led, is an idol; it has no reality. The only "reality" that could exist in this sense would be for teachers to consider themselves the ideal and then require children to become like them. Such teachers would at least touch some sort of reality, but the absurdity of saying such a thing would be obvious.

When we deal with young children, we are faced with beings who have not yet begun physical existence; they have brought down spirit and soul from pre-earthly worlds and plunged into the physical bodies provided by parents and ancestors. We see a baby before us in the first days of life, having undeveloped features and unorganized, random movements. We follow daily and weekly how the features become more and more defined and express what is struggling to the surface from the inner life of soul. We observe how the life and movements of the child become more purposeful and directed and how something of the spirit and soul is working its way to the surface from the inmost depths of that child's being. Then, filled with reverent awe, we ask: What is it that is struggling to the surface? Thus, with heart and mind, we are led back to the human being, when soul and spirit lived in the spiritual, pre-earthly world, from which this child descended into the physical world. And we might say: Little child, now that you have entered into earthly existence through birth, you are among human beings; previously, however, you were among spiritual, divine beings.

What once lived among spiritual divine beings descended to live among human beings. We see the divine manifested in the child. We have a sense of standing before an altar. But there is one difference; in religious communities, it is normal for people to bring sacrificial offerings to their altars, so that those sacrifices can ascend into the spiritual world. Now, however, we have a sense of standing before an altar turned the other way; the gods allow their grace to flow down in the form of divine spiritual beings, so that those beings, acting as messengers of the gods, may reveal what is essentially human on the altar of physical life. We see in every child the revelation of divine spiritual, cosmic laws; we see the way God creates in the world. In its highest, most significant form this is revealed in the child. Hence, every single child becomes a sacred mystery to us, because every child embodies this great question. It is not a question of how to educate children to approach some ideal that has been dreamed up; it is a question of how to nurture what the gods have sent to us in the earthly world. We come to see ourselves as helpers of the divine spiritual world, and above all we learn to ask what will happen if we approach education with this attitude of mind.

True education proceeds from exactly this attitude. The important thing is to develop our teaching on the basis of this kind of thinking. Knowledge of the human being cannot be gained unless love for humankind—in this case, love for a child—becomes the mainspring of our efforts. If this happens, then a teacher's calling becomes a priestly calling, since an educator becomes a steward who accomplishes the will of the gods in a human being. Again, it may seem as though something obvious is being said here, though in a slightly different way, but this is not the case. Indeed, the very opposite occurs in today's antisocial world order, which merely wears the outer semblance of being social. Educators pursue an "idol" for humankind, failing to see themselves as nurturers of something they must first come to understand when facing a child.

A mental attitude such as I described cannot work in an abstract way; it must work spiritually, while always keeping the practical in view. Such an attitude, however, can never be acquired by accepting theories that are unrelated and alien to life; it can be gained only when you have a sense for every expression of life and are able to go with love into all its manifestations.

There is a lot of discussion today about reforming education. Ever since the war, there has been talk of a revolution in education, and we have experienced this. Every conceivable approach has been tried, and almost everyone is concerned one way or another about how to carry out these reforms. One either approaches an institution about to be established, proposals in hand, or at least makes this or that suggestion about ways to shape education. And so it goes. There is much talk about methods of education, but do you see the kind of impression all this makes when, in an unbiased way, you look at what the various reform groups, down to the most radical, present as their educational programs? I don't know if very many people consider what sort of impression it makes when we are faced with so many programs from groups advocating for educational reform. One certainly gets the impression that people are very smart today. Indeed, all these solutions are tremendously clever. And I do not say this with irony, but quite seriously. There has never been a time when there was as much ingenuity as there is in our time.

It's all there, set out for us: *Paragraph 1.* "How to educate so that children's forces will develop naturally." *Paragraph 2.... Paragraph 3....* And so on. Today, people of any profession, occupation, or social class can sit down together and work out these programs; everything we get, in paragraphs one through thirty, will be delightfully ingenious, because we really know exactly how to form theories. People have never been so good at formulating things as they are today. Then a program, or several programs, can be submitted to a committee or legislature. This again is very resourceful. Something may be changed, deleted, or added according to party opinion, and something very ingenious emerges, even if it is sometimes strongly partisan. Nothing can be done with it, however, but this is really beside the point.

Waldorf education never began with such a program. I don't want to brag, of course, but if this had been our purpose, we could also have produced a program at least as clever as those coming from many associations for educational reform. The fact that we have to deal with reality might prove a hindrance, and so the result would be more stupid. With us, however, it has never been a matter of a program. From the very beginning, we were never interested in "educational principles" that might be incorporated into a formalized system of education. What we were really interested in was reality—absolute reality. What is this reality? First, there were children, individual children with various characteristics. We had to learn what these were and get to know the children's inherent characteristics that they had brought down with them; we had to understand what was expressed through their physical bodies.

First and foremost, then, there were the children. Then there were the teachers. You can adopt, as much as you like, the principle that children should be educated according to individuality (this is part of every reform program), but absolutely nothing will come of it. On the other hand, aside from the children, there are the teachers, and it is important to know what the teachers can accomplish with children. The school must be run in such a way that we do not establish some abstract ideal; rather, we allow the school to develop out of the teachers and students. Those teachers and students are not present in any sort of abstract way; they are very real, individual human beings. That is the gist of the matter. Then, by virtue of necessity, we are led to build up a true education based on a real knowledge of the human being. We cease to be theoretical and become practical in every detail.

Waldorf education, the first teaching method based on anthroposophy, is in reality the practice of education as an art; thus it is possible to give only indications of what can be done in various situations. We have no interest in grand theories, but so much the greater is our interest in impulses of spiritual science, which can give us real knowledge of the human being—beginning, as it must, with the child. Today, however, unrefined observation completely ignores the most important characteristics in the progressive stages of life. I would say that we must draw some inspiration from spiritual science if we wish to develop the right sense for what we should bring to children.

People today know very little about the human being and about humankind in general. People imagine that our present state of existence is the same as it was in the fourteenth or sixteenth century and, indeed, that it has never been any different. They picture the ancient Greeks or Egyptians as being pretty much the same as we are today. And, going back even further, today's views see natural scientific history enveloped in mist—to the degree that beings emerge who are half ape and half human. There is no interest, however, in penetrating the great differences between the historic and prehistoric epochs of humankind.

Let us study human beings as they appear to us today, beginning in infancy up to the change of teeth. We see very clearly that physical development runs parallel to the development of soul and spirit. Everything that manifests as soul and spirit has an exact counterpart in the physical; both appear together, both develop out of the child together. When children have gone through the change of teeth, we see how the soul is already freeing itself from the body. On the one hand, we can follow the development of soul and spirit in children and, on the other, their physical development. These two sides, however, have not yet clearly separated. If we continue to follow the development until the time between puberty and about the twenty-first year, the separation becomes much more defined, and then when we reach the twenty-seventh or twenty-eighth year (speaking now of modern humanity), we no longer see how the soul and spirit is connected with the physical body. What a person does at this age can be perceived, on the one hand, in the life of soul and spirit and, on the other hand, in the physical life; but the two cannot be connected. By the end of the twenties, a person's soul and spirit has separated completely from what is physical, and so it goes on until the end of life.

Nevertheless, this is not the way it has always been; it is merely a belief to think that it was. Spiritual science, studied anthroposophically, clearly shows us a fact that has simply not been noticed. What we see in children at the present stage of human evolution persisted, at one time, right into extreme old age; in their being of soul and spirit, children are completely dependent on the physical body, and their physical nature depends completely on their being of soul and spirit. If we go very far back, to the times that produced the concept of a "patriarch," we can ask ourselves what sort of man a patriarch was. The answer must be something like this: Such a man, in growing old, changed in terms of his physical nature, but, even at an extremely old age, he continued to feel as only very young people feel today. Even in old age he sensed that his being of soul and spirit was dependent on his physical body.

Today we no longer have the sense that our physical body depends on the way we think and feel. But in ancient times, a dependence of this kind was experienced. After a certain age of life, however, people also felt that their bones became harder and that their muscles contained certain foreign substances that brought about a hardened condition. They felt their life forces waning, but along with this physical decline they also experienced an increase of spiritual forces, brought about by the breaking up of the physical. The soul was being freed of the physical body; this is how they experienced the beginning of this process of physical decline. Having reached the age of a patriarch, the body was breaking up, and the soul was most able to free itself from the body, so that it was no longer within it. This is why people looked up to the patriarchs with such devotion and reverence. They knew how it would be for them one day in old age. In old age, one could know and understand things, penetrating to the heart of matters in a way that was not yet possible while one was still building up the physical body.

During those ancient times, one would be able to look into a world order that was both physical and spiritual. But this was in a very remote past. Then came a time when people felt this interdependence of the physical and spiritual until only around the fiftieth year. This was followed by the Greek age. The special value of the Greek epoch rests on the fact that they were able to feel the harmony between the spirit and the physical body. The Greeks felt this harmony until their thirties or forties. In the circulation of the blood, they still experienced what united the soul with the physical. The wonderful culture and art of the Greeks was based on this unity; it transformed everything theoretical into art and, at the same time, filled their art with wisdom.

In those times, sculptors worked in such a way that they had no need for models, because, in their own organization, they were aware of the forces that permeate the arms or legs, giving them form. This was learned, for example, in the festival games. Today, however, even when such games are imitated, they have no meaning.

If, however, we have a sense for the development of humankind, we know what has really taken place in human evolution. To be precise, we also know that today a parallel exists between the physical body and the spirit only until the age of twenty-seven or twenty-eight. Most people observe this parallel only until the age of puberty. Thus, we know how divine spirit springs up and grows from the developing human being. We then feel the necessary reverence for our task of developing what meets us in a child—that is, to develop what is *given* to us, not abstract, theoretical formulas.

Our thoughts are thus directed to knowledge of the human being, based on the individuality in the soul. If we absorb these universal historical aspects, we will also be able to approach every educational task in an appropriate way. In this way, another life is brought into the class when the teacher enters it; the teacher carries the world into it—the physical world and the world of soul and spirit. The teacher is thus surrounded by an atmosphere of reality, a real concept of the world, not one merely thought out and intellectual. The teacher will then be surrounded by a world imbued with feeling.

Now if we consider what has just been presented, we realize a remarkable fact. We see that we are establishing an education that, by degrees, will represent in many ways the very opposite of the characteristic impulse in education today. All sorts of comedians who have some knack for caricature frequently choose the school teacher as an object for the purpose of derision. And any teacher with the necessary sense of humor can turn the tables on those comedians—but this is not the point. Even when teachers are versed in modern educational methods and take them into school with them, if they lack the means to understand the children they must deal with, how can they be anything but strangers to the world? With the school systems we have today, one cannot be anything else; teachers are torn out of the world. We are faced, therefore, with a truly remarkable situation. Teachers are alienated from the world, but they are nevertheless expected to train human beings to go out and prosper in the world.

Let us imagine, however, that the things we have been speaking of today become an accepted viewpoint. The relationship between teachers and children is such that, in each individual child, a whole world is revealed, and not just a human world, but also a divine spiritual world manifested on earth. In other words, the teacher perceives as many aspects of the world as there are children in the class. Through each child, the teacher looks into the wide world. Thus, education becomes art. It is imbued with an awareness that whatever one does directly affects world evolution. Teaching in this sense leads teachers, in the task of educating and developing human beings, to a lofty worldview. Such teachers are those who gain the ability to play a leading role in the great questions that face civilization. The student will never outgrow such a teacher, as they so often do today.

Consider this scenario in a school. Imagine that a teacher has to educate according to some idea or preconceived image of the human being. Let's say that she has thirty children in her class. Among them are two who, through an innate capacity and guided by destiny, happen to be far more gifted than the teacher herself. What should the teacher do? She would want to shape them according with her educational ideal; anything else would be impossible. And how does this turn out? Reality does not permit it, and the students outgrow their teacher. If, on the other hand, we educate according to reality, we nurture all that manifests in children as qualities of soul and spirit. Thus, we are like gardeners with our plants. Do you think that gardeners know all the secrets of the plants they tend? Plants contain many, many more secrets than gardeners understand, but they can tend them, nevertheless, and perhaps succeed best in caring for those that they do not yet know. Their knowledge rests on practical experience, a "green thumb."

Similarly, it is possible for teachers who practice an art of education based on reality to stand as educators before children who have genius—even when they themselves are certainly not geniuses. Such teachers know that they have no need to lead students toward some abstract ideal; rather, in the children, the divine is working in the human being, right through the physical body. Teachers who have this attitude can achieve what we've just talked about. They do this through an outpouring love that permeates their work as educators. It is this mental attitude that is so essential.

With these words—offered as a kind of greeting today—I hoped to give you some idea of the essence of this lecture course. It will deal with the educational value of understanding the human being and the cultural value of education.

2 | Incarnation of the Human Being in a Physical Body

July 18, 1924

*I*n this lecture course, I want to begin by speaking about how the art of education can be advanced and enriched by an understanding of the human being. Therefore, I will approach the subject as I mentioned in my introductory lecture, when I tried to describe how anthroposophy, in a practical way, can help toward a genuine understanding the human being—not just the child, but the human being as a whole. I showed how, because spiritual science has an overall knowledge of the whole of human life from birth to death (to the degree that this takes place on earth), it can correctly show us the essentials of childhood education.

It is easy to think that we can know how to educate children by simply observing the events of childhood and youth; but this is not enough. On the contrary, it is like working with a plant; if you introduce a substance to the growing shoot, its effect shows up in the blossom or fruit. It is similar for human life; the effect of what we instill in children during the earliest years—or what we draw from them during those years—will occasionally appear in the latest years of life. It is seldom realized that, when someone develops an illness or infirmity around the age of fifty, it has been caused by incorrect methods of teaching during the person's seventh or eighth year. People today usually study the children (though perhaps less externally than I described yesterday) to discover the best ways to help them. This is not enough. Today I would like to lay some foundations on which I will show how we can observe the whole human life by means of spiritual science.

Yesterday, I said that human beings should be seen as made up of body, soul, and spirit. And I gave some indication of how it is the suprasensory nature of human beings, our higher being, that endures from birth until death, whereas the physical body's substances are always changing. It is essential, therefore, to understand human life in such a way that we see events on earth as an outcome of life before birth. We have not only the soul qualities within that began at birth or conception, but we also carry pre-earthly soul qualities—indeed, we even carry the results of previous earthly lives within us. All this is alive and active in us, and during earthly life we must prepare everything that will eventually pass through the gate of death and live again in the world of soul and spirit, beyond earthly life. Consequently, we must come to understand how the suprasensory works into earthly life, because it is present between birth and death. It acts in a hidden way within our bodily nature, and we cannot understand the body if we fail to understand the spiritual forces acting within it.

Let us now look at what I have just suggested. We can do this by considering actual examples. Anthroposophic literature such as my books *Theosophy, An Outline of Esoteric Science,* and *How to Know Higher Worlds* describe ways to understand the human being.[*] Let us begin with what leads to a true, concrete knowledge of the human being, based on anthroposophic statements about humankind and the world. I would like to give you the examples of two people who are certainly familiar to you. I chose them because I studied them both very intensely for many years. These are two men of genius; later, we will consider less gifted individuals. We will see then that anthroposophy does not speak only in general, abstract ways, but penetrates real human beings with such understanding that knowledge of the human being is shown to have practical reality for life. By choosing Goethe and Schiller as my examples, and by approaching them indirectly, I hope to show how knowledge of the human being is acquired through spiritual science.

Let us consider Goethe and Schiller, just as they appeared outwardly during their lives. In each case, we will look at the whole personality.

Goethe was an individual who entered life in a remarkable way.[†] He was born black—or, rather, dark blue. This shows how very difficult it was for his spirit to enter physical incarnation. But once this occurred and Goethe had overcome the resistance of this physical body, he was completely in it. On the one hand, it is difficult to imagine

---

[*] These three books along with *Intuitive Thinking As a Spiritual Path: A Philosophy of Freedom,* are considered Steiner's fundamental written works. Please see "Further Reading" for these and other references.

[†] Johann Wolfgang von Goethe (1749–1832) acquired knowledge of Greek, Latin, French, and Italian as a boy. At about sixteen, he began to study law. He also studied art, music, anatomy, and chemistry. Goethe's first dramatic success was *Götz von Berlichingen,* the story of a sixteenth-century robber baron. It represented his youthful protest against the establishment and a demand for intellectual freedom. The writing of Goethe's *Faust,* the best known of his works, extended throughout most of his literary life. It was finally finished when he was eighty-one.

a more healthy nature than the boy-
hood of Goethe; he was amazingly
healthy. Indeed, he was so healthy
that his teachers found him difficult.
Those who present no problem as
children seldom enjoy good health in
later life. On the other hand, children
who are a nuisance to their teachers
tend to accomplish more in later life,
because they have more active and energetic natures.
Understanding teachers, therefore, are happy when children keep a sharp eye on them.

From his earliest childhood, Goethe was inclined in this
way, even in the literal sense of the word. He watched the
fingers of someone playing the piano and then named
one finger "Thumby," another "Pointy," and so on. But
beyond this, even in childhood, he was bright and wide
awake, and this occasionally gave his teachers trouble.
Later, in Leipzig, Goethe experienced a severe illness.
Bear in mind, however, that certain difficult experiences
and sowing of wild oats were needed to bring about a
decrease in his health—to the point where he could be
attacked by the illness that he suffered in Leipzig. After
this illness, Goethe's whole life was one of robust health,
but at the same time he was extraordinarily sensitive. He
reacted strongly to all kinds of impressions, but he did
not allow them to take hold or go deeply into his organism. He did not suffer from heart trouble when deeply
moved by some experience, but he experienced any such
event intensely. His sensitivity of soul followed him
throughout life; he suffered, but his suffering was not
expressed as physical illness. Thus his bodily health was
exceptionally sound.

Furthermore, Goethe felt called upon to show restraint in his way of looking at things. He did not sink into vague mysticism or adopt the frequently held belief that there is no need to look after the outer physical form, but merely gaze at the spiritual. It was just the opposite; to one with Goethe's healthy worldview, spirit and the physical are one. He was alone in understanding that one can observe spirit through the image of the physical.

Goethe was tall when he sat, and short when he stood. When he stood you could see that he had short legs. This characteristic is especially important to those who can observe the human being as a whole. Why were Goethe's legs so short? Short legs lead to a certain way of walking. Goethe took short steps, because the upper part of his body was heavy and long, and he placed his foot firmly on the ground. As teachers, we must observe these things so that we can study them in children. Why would a person have short legs and a large upper body? This is an outward indication that, in the present earthly life, a person can harmoniously express what was experienced in a previous life on earth. Goethe was extraordinarily harmonious in this way; even in very old age, he was able to describe what lay behind his karma. Indeed, he lived to such an advanced age because he was able to bring to fruition the potential gifts of his karma.

Even after Goethe left his physical body, it was still so beautiful that those who saw him after his death were filled with wonder. Our impression is that Goethe experienced his karmic potential to the fullest extent; now nothing is left, and he must begin afresh when he enters an earthly body again under completely different conditions. This is expressed in the particular formation of a body such as Goethe's. The cause of what we bring with us as predispositions from earlier incarnations is revealed mostly in the formation of one's head. Goethe, from the time of his youth, had the beautiful head of an Apollo, from which only harmonious forces flowed down into his physical body. His body, however, was burdened by the weight of its upper part and his legs that were too short, and this led to his peculiar way of walking, which lasted throughout his life. His whole being was a wonderful, harmonious expression of his karma and karmic fulfillment. Every detail of Goethe's life illustrates this.

Such a person, living harmoniously until a ripe old age, must experience outstanding events during middle age. Goethe lived to be eighty-three. He thus reached middle age in 1790, at around forty-one years of age. If we consider the years between 1790 and 1800, we have the central decade of his life. Indeed, during that period, Goethe experienced the most important events of his life. Before that time, he found it impossible to formulate his philosophical and scientific ideas in any definite way, important though they were. *The Metamorphosis of Plants* was first published in 1790; everything related to it is connected with the decade between 1790 and 1800. In 1790, Goethe was so far from finishing *Faust* that he published it as a "fragment." At the time, he had no idea whether he would ever be able to finish it. During that decade, influenced by his friendship with Schiller, he had the bold idea of continuing *Faust*. The greatest scenes, including the "Prologue in Heaven," were from this period. Thus, in Goethe we see an exceptionally harmonious life, a life that runs its quiet course, undisturbed by inner conflict and devoted freely and contemplatively to the outer world.

By contrast, let us consider the life of Schiller.[*] From the very beginning, he was placed in a life situation that reveals disharmony between his soul and spirit and his physical body. His head lacked the harmonious formation that we find in Goethe. One could even say that he was ugly—in a way that did not hide his gifts, but ugly nonetheless. In spite of this, his strong personality revealed itself in the way he held himself, and this was also expressed in his features, especially in the formation of his nose. Schiller was not long in body, and he had long legs. On the other hand, everything between his head and limbs—in the area of circulation and breathing—was definitely sick and poorly developed from birth. He also suffered from cramps throughout his life.

At first, there were long periods between attacks, but later they became almost incessant. They became so severe, in fact, that he could not accept invitations to meals. Instead, he was forced to make it a condition that he would be invited for the whole day—for instance, when he came to Berlin on one occasion—so that he could choose a time when he was free of such pain. The cause of all this was an imperfect development of the circulatory and breathing systems.

---

[*] Friedrich von Schiller (1759–1805) wrote several plays before devoting himself to historical studies. In 1794, he established a close friendship with Goethe, who encouraged him to return to writing plays, which led to *Wallenstein's Camp*, *Mary Stuart*, *The Maid of Orleans*, *William Tell*, and others. In 1799, he moved to Weimar, where he and Goethe collaborated to make the Weimar Theater one of the finest in Germany. Schiller died of tuberculosis at the age of forty-six.

So, what is the karmic reason from a previous earthly life that causes one to suffer from painful cramps? When pains such as these take hold of one's body, they point directly to karma. If we adopt a sense of earnest scientific responsibility and attempt to investigate these cramp phenomena from the standpoint of spiritual science, we always find a specific karmic cause behind them—the results of actions, thoughts, and feelings from an earlier earthly life. We are faced with this man, and one of two things may arise. On the one hand, everything goes just as harmoniously as it did with Goethe, and we can say that we are dealing with karma; everything manifests through karma. On the other hand, because of certain conditions that result while descending from the spirit world into the physical, one meets a condition in which the burden of karma cannot be worked through completely. We descend from the spirit world with certain karmic predispositions, and we carry these in us.

Imagine that *A* in this diagram represents a specific time in the life of a man. At this point, he should be able to realize, or fulfill, his karma in some way, but for some reason this does not happen. The fulfillment of his karma is interrupted, and a period of time must pass while his karma "pauses." Fulfillment must be postponed until the next life on earth. And so it goes. Point *B* becomes another place when he should be able to fulfill his karma in some way, but again he must wait and postpone this aspect of his karma until the next incarnation.

When we are forced to interrupt karma in this way, painful cramps can appear in life, and thus we are unable to fully fashion life through through our inherent nature. This demonstrates the true nature of spiritual science. It does not indulge in fantasy, nor does it speak in vague, general terms about the four members of the human being—the physical, etheric, astral, and I beings. On the contrary, it penetrates real life and shows the true spiritual causes of various outer manifestations. It knows how we represent *ourselves* in ordinary life. This is the knowledge that real spiritual science must be able to achieve.

Now the question arises: In a life such as that of Schiller, how does karma shape the whole life if, as it happened in his case, conditions prevent karma from functioning correctly, and thus he has to make continual efforts to accomplish what he wills to do? For Goethe, it was relatively easy to complete his great works. For Schiller, the act of creation was always very difficult. He had to "attack" his karma, and the way he goes on the attack will not reveal its results until his next earthly life.

One day I had to ask myself: What is the connection between a life such as Schiller's and the more common conditions of life? If we try to answer such a question superficially, nothing significant emerges, even with the help of spiritual scientific research. We cannot spin a web of fantasy; we must observe. Nevertheless, if we approach the first object of observation in a direct way, we will become sidetracked. Thus I considered the question as follows: How does a life proceed in the presence of karmic hindrances or other pre-earthly conditions?

I then began to study certain individuals in whom something like this had already occurred. I will give you an example. There are many similar examples, but I will use one that I can describe exactly. I had an acquaintance, a person I knew very well in his present earthly life. I was able to establish that there were no hindrances in his life related to the fulfillment of karma; but there were hindrances from what had taken place in his existence between death and rebirth—that is, in the suprasensory life between his previous earthly life and the one in which I came to know him. In his case, there were not, as there were with Schiller, hindrances that prevent the fulfillment of karma. But there were hindrances that blocked his incorporation of what he experienced between death and a new birth in the suprasensory world. Observing this man, one could see that his experiences between death and a new birth had real significance, but they could not be expressed in earthly life. He had entered karmic relationships with others, and he also incarnated at a time when it was impossible to realize fully what he had "piled up" as the substance of his inner soul experience between death and conception.

So, what manifested physically because this man was unable to realize what had been presented to him in the suprasensory world? He stuttered; he had a speech impediment. If we take another step and investigate the causes working in the soul that lead to speech disturbances, we always find that there is a blockage that prevents suprasensory experiences between death and rebirth from entering the physical world through the body. Now the question arises: What is the situation for one who carries very much within him that was brought about through previous karma? It was all stored up in the existence between death and a new birth, and, because he cannot bring it into life, he becomes a stutterer. What sort of things are connected with such a person in earthly life?

Again and again, we could say that this man carries many great qualities gained during pre-earthly life, but he cannot bring them down to earth. He was able to incarnate what he could develop in forming the physical body until the change of teeth; he even had a strong ability to develop what takes place between the change of teeth and puberty. He also developed an outstanding literary and artistic capacity, because he had been able to form all that can be developed between puberty and the thirtieth year.

Now, however, for one who has true knowledge of the human being a deep concern arises, a concern that could be expressed this way: What will be the situation for this person when he enters his thirties, when he should increasingly develop a spiritual, or consciousness, soul, in addition to the intellectual, or mind, soul? Those who have knowledge of such matters will feel the deepest concern in such cases, because they can see that the consciousness soul (which develops through all that arises in the head, perfect and complete) will be unable to develop fully. For this person, the fact that he stuttered showed that something in the area of the head was not in proper order.

Apart from stuttering, this man was as completely sound—with the exception that, in addition to his stutter (which showed that not everything was in order in the head) he suffered from a squint. Again, this indicated that he had been unable to incarnate in this life all that he had absorbed in the suprasensory life between death and rebirth. One day he came to me and said, "I decided to have surgery done for my squint." I could only say, "If I were you, I would not have it done." I did everything I could to dissuade him. At the time, I did not see the whole situation as clearly as I do today; what I am describing happened more than twenty years ago. But I was very concerned about this operation.

In the end, he did not follow my advice; the operation went ahead, and this is what happened. Shortly after the operation, which was very successful (as such surgery generally is), he came to me in a happy mood and said, "Now I will not squint anymore." He was a bit vain, as distinguished people frequently are. But I was troubled. A few days later, the man died, having just completed his thirtieth year. The doctors diagnosed typhoid, but it was not typhoid; he died of meningitis.

Spiritual researchers do not need to be heartless when considering such a life. On the contrary, sympathy is deepened. One can nevertheless see through life and comprehend its manifold aspects and relationships. We perceive that spiritual experiences between death and rebirth cannot be brought into the present life and that this is expressed as physical defects. Unless the right education can intervene—which was impossible in this case—life cannot be extended beyond certain limits.

Please do not think I am implying that everyone who squints will die at thirty. Negative implications are never intended, and it certainly could happen that other karmic influences will enter life and allow such a person to live to a ripe old age. In this case, however, there was good reason to be anxious, because the demands placed on the system in the head resulted in squinting and stuttering. One had to ask: How can a person with an organization like this live beyond thirty-five? It is at this point that we must look back at a person's karma. We see immediately that it was not a given—that one who has a squint must die at thirty.

Those who have prepared themselves in pre-earthly life and have absorbed a great deal between death and a new birth may nevertheless be unable to incorporate what they received into physical life. If we consider every aspect of karma in the case I described, we find that certain individuals might very likely live beyond thirty-five. Besides all the other conditions, however, such people would have to possess an impulse that leads to a spiritual view of humankind and the world. This man had a natural disposition for spiritual matters that is rarely encountered; but despite this fact, powerful inherent spiritual impulses from previous earthly lives were too unbalanced, and he was unable to approach the spiritual.

I assure you that I can speak of such a matter. I was a close friend of that man and therefore well aware of the deep cleft between my own worldview and his. Intellectually, we could understand each other very well; we could be on excellent terms in other ways, but it was impossible to speak to him of spiritual matters. Consequently, at thirty-five he would have had to find his way into a spiritual life; otherwise his latent gifts could not be realized on earth. He died when he did because he was unable to accept a spiritual life. It is, of course, quite possible to stutter or have a squint and nevertheless continue life as an ordinary mortal. There is no cause for fear as a result of what we must say to describe realities instead of wasting our breath in mere phrases. Moreover, this example shows how observation, sharpened by spiritual insight, enables us to look deeply into human life.

Now let us return to Schiller. When we consider his life, two things strike us most of all, because they are so remarkable. There is an unfinished drama by Schiller, only a sketch. The title of that work is *Die Malteser* ("The

Maltese").* We see from the concept behind this sketch that, if Schiller had wanted to complete his drama, he could have done so only as one who had experienced initiation. It could not have been finished otherwise. To a certain degree, at least, he had the inner qualities needed for initiation, but because of other karmic conditions, these qualities could not get through; they were suppressed, or cramped. There was a cramping of his soul life, too, and this can be seen in his sketch of the *Die Malteser*. There are long powerful sentences that never come to a full stop. Whatever is in him cannot find a way out.

It is interesting to observe that, for Goethe, too, we have unfinished sketches such as this, but, in his case, when he left something unfinished, he did so because he was too easy-going to carry it any further; he could have finished it. This would have proved impossible for him only at a very advanced age, after sclerosis had set in. For Schiller, however, we see another picture. He had an iron will when he tried to develop the *Die Malteser*, but he could not do it. He could write only a slight sketch, because his drama, in reality, contains something that, since the time of the Crusades, has been preserved in the various kinds of occultism, mysticism, and initiation science. Schiller went to work on this kind of drama, but to complete it he would have had to experience initiation.

This is truly a life's destiny that deeply moves those who are able to look behind such things and see into the real being of the person. Once it became known that Schiller intended to write a drama such as *Die Malteser*, there was a tremendous increase in opposition to him in

---

* Friedrich Schiller's incomplete work, *Die Malteser*, was a dramatic tragedy based on the Turkish siege of Malta in 1530.

Germany. He was feared. People feared that he might betray all kinds of occult secrets in his drama.

I also want to say something about another work. Schiller was unable to finish *Die Malteser;* he could not get through it. He let time slip by, and he wrote all sorts of things that certainly warrant admiration, but these can be admired by any "philistine." If he had been able to complete *Die Malteser,* it would called for the attention of individuals with the most powerful and vigorous minds. But he had to set it aside.

After some time, he received a new impulse that inspired his later work. He could no longer think about *Die Malteser,* but began to compose *Demetrius.* It portrays a remarkable problem of destiny, the story of the false *Demetrius* who takes the place of another man. To complete this story, Schiller would have to include all the story's conflicting destinies, emerging from hidden causes, and all the human emotions thus aroused. As he went to work on it with feverish activity, people became aware of it and were even more afraid that certain things would be exposed, and they had an interest in keeping such matters hidden from the rest of humankind for some time yet.

And now certain things occurred in Schiller's life that, for those who understand them, cannot be attributed to an ordinary illness. We have a remarkable picture of this illness; something tremendous happened—not just in terms of its severity, but also in its shattering force. Schiller became ill while writing *Demetrius.* In a raging fever on his sick bed, he continually repeated almost all of *Demetrius.* It seemed as though an alien power was at work in him, expressing itself through his body. There is no ground for accusing anyone, of course, but, despite everything written about this, we must look at the whole picture of this illness and conclude that, one way or another—even in an essentially occult way—*something* contributed to the rapid culmination of Schiller's illness in death. We know that some people suspected this because Goethe, who was unable to do anything but suspect, refrained from participating personally in any way during Schiller's final days—not even after his death, although he felt it deeply. He did not dare to make his inner thoughts known.

These remarks are intended only to point out that, for anyone who can see through such things, Schiller was undoubtedly predestined to create works of a high spiritual order, but because of inner and outer karmic reasons, it was all held back, "dammed up," within him. I venture to say that, for spiritual investigators, there is nothing more interesting than to study Schiller's achievements during the final ten years of his life—from the *Aesthetic Letters* on—and then to follow the course of his life after death. A deep penetration of Schiller's soul after death reveals manifold inspirations coming to him from the spirit world. This is why Schiller had to die in his mid-forties. His condition of cramps and his build as a whole, especially the ugly formation of his head, made it impossible for him to incarnate physically the essence of his soul and spirit, which was deeply rooted in spiritual existence.

Bearing such things in mind, we must acknowledge that the study of human life is deepened through the use of what spiritual science provides. We learn to see right into human life. In presenting these examples to you, my sole purpose was to show how one learns through anthroposophy to contemplate the life of human beings.

Let us now look at the matter as a whole. Can't we deepen our feeling and understanding for everything human just by looking at an individual human life, as we have done here? At a certain moment in life, if we can say: This is how it was for Schiller and Goethe and for the other young man I told you about; doesn't this stir something within our souls, teaching us to look at every child in a deeper way? Doesn't every human life become a sacred mystery to us? Will we learn to contemplate every human life, every human being, with much more inner attention? And, because knowledge of the human being is instilled into our souls in this way, can't we deepen our love for humankind? And with this human love, doesn't our study of the human being give depth to the innermost sacred mystery of life, and with this love, won't we be able to truly enter the task of education because life itself has became sacred to us? Won't the teacher's purpose be transformed from mere ideological phrases and dreamlike mysticism into a truly sacred calling, ready to do its work when divine grace sends human beings into earthly life?

Everything depends on the development of such feelings. The essence of spiritual science is not mere theoretical teaching; we don't merely learn that human beings consist of physical, etheric, astral, and I beings or that there are laws of karma, reincarnation, and so on. People can be very bright and know everything; but these are not anthroposophists in the true sense of the word, just because they know these things in an ordinary way, as one might learn the contents of a cookbook. The important thing is for the life of human souls to be enlivened and deepened by the spiritual scientific worldview, and that we learn to work and act from a soul life that has been deepened and made alive.

This is the first task in fostering education that is based on anthroposophy. From the very beginning, one should work in such a way that teachers and educators know the human being in the deepest sense, so that out of the conviction that arises from observing human beings correctly, they approach children with love that is born from such thinking. And so it follows that, when teachers train to work in an anthroposophic way, we do not begin by saying you should do it like this or like that, or you should use this or that educational trick. First we awaken a true educational sense, born from our knowledge of the human being. If we have been successful in awakening this real love of education in teachers, then we can say that they are ready to begin their work as educators.

In education based on knowledge of the human being, as is Waldorf education for example, the first thing to consider is not conveying rules or advice about how one is supposed to teach; the first thing is to hold training courses for teachers in such a way that we find the hearts of the teachers and deepen those hearts so that love for the children grows from them. It is natural for teachers to believe that they can "impose" such love on themselves, but imposed human love achieves nothing. There may be good intentions behind it, but it will achieve nothing. The only human love that can do anything arises from a deepened observation of individual cases.

If you really wish to develop an understanding of the essential principles of education based on knowledge of the human being—whether you have already gained knowledge of spiritual science or, as also happens, you have an intuitive grasp of such matters—you will observe children in such a way that you are faced with a question: What is the main thrust of a child's development up to the change of teeth? An intimate study of the human being reveals that, up to the change of teeth, children are completely different from what they become later on. A tremendous inner transformation takes place at this time, and another tremendous transformation occurs at puberty.

Just consider what this change of teeth means for growing children. It is only the outer indication of deep changes that take place in the whole human being, changes that occur only once; we get our second teeth only once, not every seven years. With the change of teeth, the formative process in the teeth ends. After this, we retain our teeth throughout life. The most we can do is have them filled or replace them with false ones, because our organism will not produce more. The reason for this is that, with the change of teeth, the organization of the head is brought to a certain conclusion. If we are aware of this in each case and ask ourselves what is really being concluded with the change of teeth, we are led at this point to comprehend the whole human organization of body, soul, and spirit. And if we observe a child up to the change of teeth—with our view deepened by love gained through a knowledge of the human being, as I have described—we see that it is during these years that children learn to walk, speak, and think. These are the three most outstanding faculties that are developed up to the change of teeth.

Walking involves more than just learning to walk. Walking is only one manifestation of what actually takes place; it means learning to adapt to the world by gaining a sense of balance. Walking is only the most obvious expression of this process. Before learning to walk, children do not need equilibrium in the world, but now they learn this. How does it come about? It happens because we are born with a head that requires a certain position in relation to the forces of balance. We can see the secret of the human head very clearly in the physical body. Bear in mind that the average human brain weighs between one and one and a half kilograms. If this much weight were to press down on the delicate veins at the base of the brain, it would quickly crush them. This is prevented because the weight of the brain floats in the cerebral fluid that fills the head. No doubt you recall from your studies in physics that a body floating in a fluid loses weight in proportion to the fluid that it displaces. Apply this to the brain and you discover that our brain presses on its base with a weight of around twenty grams; the remaining weight is lost in the cerebral fluid. Thus, at birth the brain is positioned so that its weight will be in correct proportion to the displaced cerebral fluid. This is adjusted when we lift ourselves from crawling to an upright posture. The position of the head must now be brought into relationship to the rest of the organism. Walking and using our hands require the head to assume a certain position. Our sense of balance proceeds from the head.

Let's take this a step further. At birth, our head is relatively highly organized; until then, it is formed in the embryo, though it will not become fully developed until the change of teeth. It is the rhythmic system that is first established during the time before the change of teeth, when it receives its special outer organization. If you simply observe physiological processes more carefully, you can see the importance of establishing the circulatory and breathing systems during the first seven years. Above all, you recognize how much damage can be done if the physical life of a child does not develop properly. We must face the fact, therefore, that in these first years of life something is at work that is now establishing its own laws in the circulatory and breathing systems. Children sense unconsciously how their life forces work in their circulation and breathing. A physical organ such as the brain must establish a state of balance; likewise, the soul in the first years of life plays a role in the development of the rhythmic systems. The physical body must actively bring about a state of balance proceeding from the head. The soul, to the degree that it is organized correctly for this purpose, must be active in the changes in the circulation and breathing. Our upright bearing and the use of our hands and arms are related to what is expressed in the brain; similarly, speech develops in us in a way that is related to the systems of circulation and breathing.

By learning to speak, we establish a relationship with our circulation and breathing. In the same way, we establish a relationship between walking and dexterity and the forces of the head by learning to hold the head so that the brain loses the correct amount of weight. If you learn to perceive these relationships and then meet someone with a clear, high voice, particularly well-suited to reciting hymns or odes, or even to moral harangues, you can be certain that this is related to certain conditions of the circulatory system. Or if you meet someone with a rough, harsh voice, like beating sheets of brass and tin, you may be sure that this, too, is connected with the breathing or circulatory systems.

But there is more to it than this. When we learn to listen to a child's voice, whether harmonious and pleasant or harsh and discordant, and when we understand that this is related to movements of the lungs and to the blood circulation—movements inwardly vibrating through the whole person right into the fingers and toes—we know that this speech expresses something imbued with soul qualities. And now something like a "higher being" appears, finding expression in this image that relates speech to the physical processes of circulation and breathing.

Beginning with this, we can look up and see into the prenatal human life that is subject to the conditions we claimed between death and a new birth. What one experienced in pre-earthly conditions plays a role here, and so we can see that, if we are to comprehend the human being by means of true human understanding and knowledge, we must train to hear spiritually when we listen to children's voices. Then we know how to help a child whose strident voice betrays the fact that there is same kind of karmic obstruction, and we can do something to free that child from those karmic hindrances.

All this enables us to see what is needed in education— nothing less than knowledge of the human being. This is not merely the kind of knowledge that recognizes a gifted child or which children are "good" or "bad." This kind of knowledge follows up what a human being carries—for example, what is present spiritually in speech, tracing it right into the physical body, so that you are not faced with abstract spirituality but the kind of spirituality that is expressed in the physical image of a human being. Then, as teachers, you can work in such a way that you consider both spirit and body and, thus, can help the physical provide the right foundation for spirit. Furthermore, you might observe a child from behind and see that the legs are short, that the upper body is too heavy, and that this makes the child's walk too heavy, and thus, if you have acquired the right way of looking at these things, you recognize that the child's former earthly life and karma are speaking. Or you may see another expression of karma in someone who walks as did the German philosopher Johann Gottlieb Fichte, for example, who always walked with his heels placed firmly first; even when he spoke, it seemed as though the words came out "heel first."

Thus we come to recognize karma in children through observation based on spiritual science. This is extremely important, and we must investigate and understand it. Our single aid as teachers is our ability to observe human beings, to observe the children's bodies, their souls, and their spirits. In this way, knowledge of the human being must make itself felt in education, and this knowledge must be deepened in soul and spirit.

With this lecture I wanted to invoke a picture that gives an idea of what we are trying to achieve in education. It can arise in the way of practical educational results, though many people consider it to be very impractical and fantastic daydreaming.

3 | Walking, Speaking, Thinking

July 19, 1924

You may have gathered from my remarks during the past two days that a fundamental change takes place within a human being at every stage of life. Today, certainly, modern psychologists and physiologists also take this into consideration. They, too, deal with these life changes: first, the period before the change of teeth, then up to puberty, and again from puberty into the twenties. These changes, however, are more profound than we can discover through ordinary observation, which does not go far enough, however excellent one's means may be. We must go further and examine these changes from the perspectives required by spiritual science.

You will hear much that is already familiar to you, but now you must go into them more deeply. Even when a child enters this world from the embryo—looking at it externally—and adapts to the outer process of breathing, even then the child is not yet received physiologically by the outer world; this requires the natural nourishment of the mother's milk. At this stage, children are not yet nourished by what meets them from the outer world, but by what comes from the same source as the children themselves. People today study the substances they encounter in the world, more or less according to the physical, chemical properties alone, and they do not consider the finer attributes that they possess through their spiritual essence. Everything today is viewed in this way. We do not condemn such methods—on the contrary, we must recognize them as appropriate. Nevertheless, the time came when people were concerned only with the external aspects of phenomena. This was impossible in earlier times, but now we have reached a point of extreme externalization. For the sake of comparison, phenomena are observed today somewhat like this: people say, "I see death and dying; plants die, animals die, human beings die." But we must ask whether dying—the passing of the various forms of life around us—is the same for all three kinds of living beings, or whether this is merely an external appearance. Consider a few comparisons. If I have a knife, there is a big difference between cutting food with it and using it to shave. In either case, it's still a knife, but the qualities of "knife" must be differentiated further. This is often ignored today. The ways that a plant, animal, or human being die are not differentiated.

We encounter this phenomenon in other areas as well. There are those who, in a sense, want to be natural philosophers, and because their aim is to be idealistic, even spiritual, they assert that plants very likely have souls; they try to ascertain, in an external way, the characteristics of plants seem to indicate certain soul qualities. For example, they study plants that tend to open their petals when approached by insects. The insect is caught, having been attracted by the scent in a plant such as the Venus flytrap. It snaps its petals closed, and the insect is trapped. This is thought to be a soul quality in the plant.

But there is something else that works in the same way, and it can be found in all sorts of places. A mouse approaches it and is attracted by the smell of a dainty morsel; it begins to nibble, and the mousetrap snaps closed. If we were to use of the same thought process as that used in the case of a plant, we might say that the mousetrap has a soul.

This kind of thinking, although legitimate in certain situations, never leads to conclusions of any depth, but remains more or less on the surface. If we desire true knowledge of the human being, we must penetrate to the very depths of human nature. We must be able to look in a completely unbiased way at phenomena that appear paradoxical compared to an external view of things. Moreover, we must consider everything that, together, constitutes the entire human organization.

First of all, like all earthly beings—especially those of the mineral kingdom—as human beings, we have a physical organism. Nevertheless, we must clearly distinguish between our physical body and our etheric organism, which we have in common only with the plant world—not with the minerals. A being having only an etheric organism, however, cannot experience feelings nor acquire an inner consciousness. For this purpose, human beings have an astral organism, which we have in common with the world of animals. This might seem like an external organization, but in these lectures you will see how inward this can be. In addition to this, human beings have an I being, which cannot be found in the animal world; we alone possess this among earthly beings. What we are speaking of is in no way merely an outer, intellectual pattern. Further, when we use the term *ether body* (or *life body*), this is completely unrelated to the outmoded terms *life force, vital force,* and so as used in natural science. Rather, it is the result of observation.

If we study a child before the change of teeth, for example, we see that development depends mostly on the physical organism. The physical body must adapt gradually to the outer world, not all at once, even in the crudest physical sense. The physical body contains what we bring from the spirit world before earthly existence, and it cannot immediately assimilate the material of the outer world, but receives specially prepared mother's milk. A child must remain closely connected, so to speak, with another being of like nature, growing only gradually into the outer world. This process of growing physically into the outer world is indicated by the appearance of the second teeth around the seventh year, when the child's physical organism completes the process.

During this time, when the organization is concerned mainly with forming the skeletal system, children are interested in only certain things in the outer world. They are interested only in what we might call "gesture," or everything related to movement. Now consider the fact that, initially, a child's consciousness is dreamlike and shadowy; perceptions are vague, and they light up and only gradually gain clarity. Fundamentally, however, the fact remains that, in the time between birth and the change of teeth, a child's perception adheres to everything related to gesture and movement; it does so to the extent that, at the very moment when they perceive a movement, they feel an inner urge to imitate it. This is a definite law of development in human nature, which I would like to describe for you.

While growing into the physical, earthly world, inner

human nature is developing in such a way that it proceeds initially from gesture and from the differentiation of movement. Within the organism, speech develops from all the aspects of movement, and thought develops from speech. This law has deep meaning and forms the basis of all human development. Everything that appears as sound, or speech, is the result of gesture, mediated through the inner nature of the human organism.

If you turn your attention to the way a child not only learns to speak, but also learns to walk, placing one foot after the other, you can see how one child steps more strongly on the heel, and another more on the toes. You can observe children who, while learning to walk, tend to bring their legs well forward and how others are more inclined to hold back, as it were, between steps. It is very interesting to watch a child learning to walk. You must learn to observe this. And it is even more interesting, although it is given less attention, to see the way a child learns to grasp and to move the hands. There are children who, when they want something, move their hands in such a way that the fingers move as well. Others keep their fingers still and reach out to grasp without moving their fingers. Some children stretch out their hand and arm, keeping the upper body motionless; others immediately allow the upper body to follow the movement of arm and hand. I once knew a child who was very small, and when his high chair was placed at a distance from the table and some dish he wished to reach, he would "row" himself toward it; his whole body was moving. His whole body moved with every movement he made.

This is the first thing to look for in a child: the way a child moves reveals the innermost, primal life urges. At the same time, a tendency to adapt to others appears in children's movements, as they try to perform the same movements as the father, mother, or other family member. This principle of imitation is revealed in gestures and movements. Gesture appears first in human evolution. In the special human constitution of physical, soul, and spiritual organisms, gesture is transformed inwardly into speech. Those who can see this, know without doubt that children who speak as though sentences were being hacked out of them are the ones who place their heels down first. On the other hand, children who speak in such a way that sentences run into one other tend to step more on their toes. Children who take hold of things more lightly with their fingers tend to emphasize vowels, whereas those who tend to stress the consonants also tend to use the whole arm when grasping. We receive very definite impressions of children's potentials from the ways they speak.

Understanding of the world through the senses and thought is also developed out of speech. Thought does not produce speech, but the other way around. This is the way it is for the cultural development of humanity as a whole; human beings spoke first, then thought. So it is for children; first they learn to speak and articulate out of movement, then thinking arises from speech. We must therefore see this sequence as something important: gesture, speech, thought, and thinking.

This is all especially typical of the first period of a child's life, up to the change of teeth. Gradually, children grow into the world during their first to fourth years of life, and they do so through gesture; everything depends on gesture. In fact, I would suggest that speaking and thinking occur unconsciously for the most part; they develop naturally out of gesture—even the first gesture.

Therefore, we might say: From the first year to the seventh, gesture dominates the life of a child—gesture in the broadest sense of the word, which lives in a child as imitation. As educators, we must keep this firmly in mind, because up to the change of teeth children takes in only what meets them as gesture; they shut themselves off from all else. If we tell children how to do various things, they really do not hear or take any notice. But when we stand in front of them and demonstrate a way to do something, they are able to imitate the action. Children act according to the way I move *my* fingers, or they look at something just as I look at it, not according to what I say. They imitate everything. This is the secret of development in children up to the change of the second teeth. They live completely through imitation of what comes to meet them from outside as gesture, in the widest possible sense.

This accounts for the surprises we experience when teaching very young children. A father came to me once and said, "What can I do? Something terrible has happened; my boy has been stealing." I said, "First, let's find out whether he really steals. What did he do?" The father told me that the boy had taken money out of the cupboard and bought candy, which he shared with the other boys. I replied, "I presume that the boy has often seen his mother taking money from that cupboard before going shopping. It is quite natural that he would imitate her." This was confirmed, so I said, "That is not stealing; it is a natural principle of development in the boy before the change of teeth. He imitates what he sees; he must do so."

In the presence of children, therefore, we should avoid doing anything they should not imitate. This is how we educate them. If we tell them not do something, it has absolutely no influence on a child before the change of teeth. It might have some effect if you clothe the words in a kind of gesture, perhaps saying: Now you have done something that I would never do. This is a kind of disguised gesture.

It comes down to this: With our whole humanity we should fully understand how, up to the change of teeth, children are imitating beings. During this time, there is indeed an inner connection between children and their surroundings and everything happening around them. Later on, this is lost. This may sound strange and paradoxical to many today, because they are unable to think correctly about spirit and think only in abstractions. Nevertheless, it is true that the relationship between children and gesture has an innate religious quality. Through the physical body, children are given over to everything that has the quality of gesture; they cannot do other than yield themselves to it. Later on, with our soul, and even later with our spirit, we give ourselves to the divine—even to the external world—as once again spiritualized. This is what children do with the physical body when they bring it into movement. They are completely immersed in religion, with both their good and their bad qualities. Also present in a child's physical organism is what remains with us as soul and spirit later in life. Consequently, although children may not understand the inner causes of what they see, they experience something immoral when they live in close proximity to a surly, bearish father who is likely to give in to rages, who is often irritable and angry and expressing uncontrolled emotions in the children's presence.

Children perceive, however unconsciously, the moral nature of such outbreaks, so that they not only have the outer image of the gesture, but they also absorb its moral significance. If I make an angry gesture, this passes into the blood system of the child, and if these gestures occur frequently, they find expression in the child's circulation. The physical body of children is organized according to the way I behave in their presence, according to the kinds of gestures I make. Furthermore, if I fail to provide love and understanding when children are present—if, without thinking of them, I do something that is suitable only at a later age, and if I am not constantly on the watch when they are nearby—it may happen that they lovingly get into something that is unsuited to their tender years, but belongs to another age, and the physical body will be organized accordingly.

Those who study the whole course of a person's life from birth to death—keeping in mind the requirements I have mentioned—will realize that children who are exposed to things suitable only to adults and who imitate such things will later on, after the age of about fifty, suffer from sclerosis. We must be able to examine such phenomena in all their ramifications. Illnesses that appear in later life are often merely the result of educational errors made during the earliest years of childhood.

This is why an education based on a knowledge of the human being must study human nature as a whole, from birth until death. To be able to look at a person as a whole is the very essence of spiritual science. You also discover how strong the connection is between children and their surroundings. I would go so far as to say that children's souls go right out into their surroundings; they experience those surroundings intimately and have a much stronger relationship to them than during later periods of life. In this sense, children are still very close to the animal, except that they experience things in a more spiritual way and in a way more permeated with soul. An animal's experiences are coarser and cruder, but animals, too, are related to their environment.

This is why many phenomena of recent times remain unexplained; people are unable to go into all the details involved. There is, for example, the case of the "calculating horses," which have made such a stir recently. These are horses that do simple arithmetic by stamping their hooves. I have not seen the famous Elberfelder horses, but I have seen the one belonging to Herr von Osten. This horse performed addition. For instance, von Osten would ask the horse for the answer to 5 + 7. Von Osten would begin to count with 1, and when he got to 12, the horse would stamp its foot. It could add, subtract, and so on. Now there happened to be a young professor who studied the matter and wrote a very interesting book about it. In this book he claims that the horse was able to see certain little gestures made by von Osten, who would always stand close to the horse. In his opinion, when von Osten counts up to 12 and the horse stamps, this is because of a very slight gesture from von Osten when he reaches 12, and the horse, noticing this, stamps his hoof. He believes that it can all be traced back to something visible. But then he asks: Why can't you see this gesture made so skillfully that the horse sees it and stamps at the number 12? The young professor continues by saying that the gestures are so slight that, as a human being, he cannot see them. This conclusion might lead us to think that a horse sees more than a professor.

But I was unconvinced. I saw this wonderful, intelligent horse, the clever Hans, standing next to von Osten in his long coat. I saw, too, that in von Osten's right pocket he had lumps of sugar, and during his experiments with the horse he handed it one lump after another, which aroused a feeling in the horse that associated sweets with von Osten. In this way, a sort of love was established between the man and the horse. Only when this is present—only when the inner being of the horse is merged, as it were, with the inner being of von Osten through the flow of sweetness between them—only then could the horse "calculate," since it really did receive something, not through gesture, but through von Osten's thinking. He thinks "$5 + 7 = 12$," and by means of suggestion, the horse takes up this thought and even has a distinct impression of it. One can actually see this happening. The horse and master are, in a way, merged in feeling one into the other; they impart something to each other reciprocally while united through the medium of sweetness. So the animal has this finer relationship to its environment, and this can be stimulated externally—in this case, by means of sugar.

In a delicate way, children have a similar relationship to the outer world. It lives in them and needs to be addressed. Kindergarten education should rely on the principle of imitation *exclusively*. Kindergarten teachers must sit with the children and do only what they wish the children to do, so that the they simply have to imitate the teacher. All education before the change of teeth must be based on this principle.

After the change of teeth, this changes, and a child's soul life is completely different. Children now perceive more than single gestures; they see how gestures work together. For example, previously children had a sense of only a certain line; now they have a feeling for coordination, or symmetry. A feeling is awakened for whether something is coordinated, and a child's soul acquires the ability to perceive formative qualities. Once this perception is awakened, an interest in speech is simultaneously awakened. During the first seven years of life, there is an interest in gesture and everything related to movement. During the time between seven and fourteen, there is an interest in everything related to image, and speech is primarily pictorial and formative.

After the change of teeth, children's interest shifts from gesture to speech, and in the early school years, between seven and fourteen, it is best to work with everything involved in speech, and, above all, through the moral element behind speech. Before this age, children have a "religious" attitude toward the gestures they encounter in the surrounding world; now that their "religious" feeling has gradually refined into a soul experience, they relate in a moral way to everything they encounter through speech.

So, during this period of children's life, we must work with them through speech. And however we work with them, we must do so by means of unquestioned authority. When I want to communicate an image expressed through speech, I must do so with the assurance of authority. I must be the unquestioned authority for that child whenever I want to invoke an image through speech. With the smaller children, we want to show them what to do; now we must become the human pattern for children between the change of teeth and puberty. In other words, there really is no point in reasoning with children at this age, trying to make them see why something should be done or not, just because there are good reasons for or against it. This goes right over children's heads.

It is important to understand this. During the earliest

years of life, children observe only the gesture; likewise, between the change of teeth and puberty, they observe only what I, as a human being, am in relation to them. At this age, children must learn, for example, about morality in such a way that they naturally accept the authority of the teacher, so that anything designated good through speech is deemed good by the children. Whatever this authority designates as bad, the children should also consider bad. They must learn that everything their teacher does, as the authority, is good; what the teacher does not do is bad. Relatively speaking, the child feels that if the teacher says something is good, it is good; if the teacher says something is bad, it is bad.

You will not credit me with a view that maintains a principle of authority as the single means of salvation, given that I wrote *Intuitive Thinking As a Spiritual Path* [*Die Philosophie der Freiheit*] thirty years ago. Nevertheless, by knowing the true nature of freedom, we also know that, between the change of teeth and puberty, children need to be faced with an unquestioned authority; it is part of human nature. Everything in education that ignores this relationship between children and the unquestioned authority of a teacher is bound to fail. Children must be guided in everything that they should or should not do, think or not think, feel or not feel, according to what flows to them by way of speech from the teacher. Thus, at this age there is no point in approaching children through the intellect. Everything must be directed toward the life of feeling, because feeling is receptive to images, and children at this age are constituted in such a way that they live in a world of pictures, and they have the sense of welding separate details into a harmonious whole. This is one reason why

morality cannot be presented to children through precepts, or by saying that they should do this or not do
that. It just doesn't work. What does work is when children, by the way we speak to them, feel an affinity in
their souls for what is good and a dislike toward what is
bad. Between the change of teeth and puberty, children
are aesthetes, and we must make sure that they experience pleasure in the good and displeasure in everything
bad. This is the best way for children to develop a sense
of morality.

We must also be sincere inwardly in the imagery we
use with children. This means being permeated to the
core of our being by whatever we do. This is not the case
when one stands in front of children and immediately
experiences a slight sense of superiority, imagining that
one is much smarter than the children. This attitude
destroys all education; it also destroys any feeling for
authority in the children. How, then, should I create an
image out of what that I want to communicate to the children? I have chosen an example that illustrates this.

We cannot speak to children about the immortality of
the soul as we would to adults. Nevertheless, we must
convey some understanding of it, and we must do it in a
pictorial way. We should build up a picture such as this,
which might well take up a whole lesson. We explain to
the children what a butterfly's chrysalis is; then we say
something like this: Later on, the finished butterfly flies
out of the chrysalis. It was inside all the time, but it was
not yet visible; it was not ready to fly away, but it was
already present inside. Now we can go on and tell the
children that, similarly, the human body contains a soul,
which is invisible. At death, our soul flies out of the body;
here, the only difference between a human being and a

butterfly is that the butterfly is visible and the human soul is invisible.

This is how we might describe the soul's immortality to children in order to give them a true image of immortality—one that is especially suited to their age. Whenever you are with children, however, you must avoid any sense of being smart or a philosopher, and you should have absolutely no thought that, whereas you may understand the truth of immortality, the children are naive or simple and need the image of a butterfly creeping out of its chrysalis. If you think in this way, you cannot really connect with the children, and , consequently, they will get nothing at all from what they are told. The only way is to genuinely *believe* in the picture yourself; you must never want to be smarter than the children but, instead, stand in their presence just as full with belief as they are. How can you do this?

As students of spiritual science, we know that an emerging butterfly is a true image of the immortal human soul, which is placed into the world by the gods. We have to imagine that the gods inscribed this picture into the world—that is, the emerging butterfly being an image of the human soul's immortality. We see the higher processes abstracted in all the lower stages of the process. An imponderable relationship arises between you and the students; and the children make real progress in their education as long as you do not get the idea that they are ignorant and you are clever; you must stand before the children, aware that this is a fact in the world, and that you are leading them to believe in something that you yourself believe with all your heart. This is how moral imponderables continually enter the educational relationship. This is crucial.

If we are clear about this, the whole focus of our studies leads us to see how we find the right approach to education, one that is truly instructional and teaches. For example, how should children learn to read and write? There is really a lot more misery connected with this than people typically imagine, though intellectuals are far too superficial to see it. We recognize that learning to read and write is necessary, so it follows that children must be driven to learn reading and writing at all costs. Just consider, however, what this means for the child. Once children become adults, they are not the least inclined to place themselves in the children's position and imagine what they experience as they learn to read and write. In today's civilization, we have letters, *a*, *b*, *c*, and so on; they present themselves to us in definite forms. The children have the sound "ah." When do they use it? To them, this sound expresses an inner soul experience. They use this sound when faced with something that invokes a feeling of wonder, or astonishment. They understand this sound; it is connected with human nature. Or they have the sound "eh." When do they use this sound? They use it when they have the feeling that something has come up against them; they have experienced something that encroaches on their own nature. If somebody hits me, I say "eh." And it is the same for the consonants. Every sound corresponds to an expression of life; consonants imitate an external world, and the vowels express inner soul experiences. Today's study of human speech, or philology, approaches only the first aspects of these things.

Scholars who devote themselves to researching language have given much thought to the course of human evolution and the possible origins of speech. There are two theories. One represents the view that speech may have arisen from soul experiences in much the same way that this takes place in animals, albeit in the most primitive form: "moo" being the expression of what a cow feels inwardly, and "bow wow" the experience of a dog. Thus, in a more complex way, human speech arises from an urge to express inner feelings and experiences. In a somewhat humorous vein, this has been called the "bow-wow theory."

The other view comes from the supposition that, in the sounds of speech, people imitate events in the outer world. It is possible to imitate the sound of a bell, or what takes place in a bell: "ding dong, ding dong." This is an attempt to imitate what takes place in the outer world. It is the basis for the theory that everything in speech can be traced back to external sounds or events. It is the "ding dong theory."

So we have these two opposite theories. It is certainly not my intention to make fun of this; in fact, both theories are correct. The bow-wow theory is right about the vowel element in speech, and the ding dong theory is right about the consonants. By transposing gestures into sounds, through the consonants we learn to imitate outer processes inwardly; in the vowels, we form the inner experiences of the soul. In speech, the inner and the outer are united. Human nature itself is homogeneous and understands how to accomplish this.

We take children into our primary school. Because of their inner organization, they have become beings who can speak. Now, they are suddenly expected to experience (I use the word *experience* deliberately, weighing my words, not *recognize*) a connection between astonishment or wonder and a demonic sign, the letter *a*. This is completely alien to them. The children are expected to learn something that they experience as completely remote, and to relate this to the sound "ah." This is outside the comprehension of young children. They feel it as a kind of torture when we confront them from the very beginning with the forms of the letters as used today.

We can nevertheless recall something else. The letters that we use today were not always present. Let us look back to the ancient people who used a pictorial form of writing. They used images to give tangible form to what was spoken, and those pictures were certainly related in some way with what they were intended to express. They did not have the kinds of letters we use, but images related to their meaning. Until a certain time, the same could be said of cuneiform writing. In those times, people still had a relationship to phenomena, even those fixed in a definite form. We no longer have this relationship, but with children, we must return to it. Of course, we shouldn't do this by studying the cultural history of those ancient people, falling back on forms that were once used in picture writing. Rather, as teachers we must use all our educational imagination to create the pictures we need.

Fantasy, or imagination, is absolutely necessary, since we cannot teach without it. Likewise, it is always necessary to speak of the importance of enthusiasm, or inspiration, when dealing with some characteristic feature of spiritual science. It never gives me any pleasure, for example, when I enter a class in our Waldorf school and notice that the teacher is tired and merely teaching in a certain mood of weariness. We must never do this; we simply cannot be tired, but must always be filled with enthusiasm. When teaching, we must be absolutely present with our whole being. It is wrong to be tired when teaching; tiredness must be reserved for some other time. It is essential for teachers to learn how to give full play to fantasy. What do I mean by this?

First of all, I evoke in the children something that they have all seen at the store or some other place—a fish, for example. Then I get the children to draw a fish, and I even allow them to use colors, so that they paint as they would draw, and draw just as they paint. I then have them say the word *fish*, not saying the word quickly, but separating the sounds, "ff-ii-ssh." Then I lead them to say only the beginning of the word *fish* ("fff"), gradually transferring the shape of a fish into a sign that is  somewhat fishlike, while also getting them to say "f." And there we have it, the letter *f*.

Or I have the children slowly say "wave," picturing for them, at the same time, a wave. Again, I ask them to paint this and have them speak the beginning of the word, "w," and then I change the picture of a wave into the letter *w*.

Continuing in this way, I allow the written characters to emerge gradually from the painted drawing, or drawn painting, as indeed they actually arose in the first place. I do not bring the children into a stage of civilization with which they still have nothing in common; instead, I guide 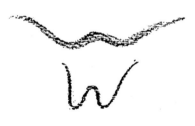 them so that they are never torn out of their relationship to the world around them. To do this, there is no need to study cultural history, even though today's writing did arise from pictorial writing. We must only allow free play in our imagination, for then we bring the children to the point where they can form writing from their drawing and painting.

Now, we must not consider this merely an ingenious, clever new method. We must value the fact that the children unite themselves inwardly with something new to them while their soul activity is constantly stimulated. They do not "grow into it" when they are forced and always entering unfamiliar relationships with their surroundings. The whole point is to work on the inner being of the children.

What do people usually do today? Maybe it is already somewhat dated, but not long ago people gave little girls "beautiful" dolls, with real hair, with pretty faces, with eyes that close when the dolls are laid down, and so on. Modern society considers them beautiful, but they are hideous, because they show no artistic qualities. What sort of dolls are these? They are dolls that cannot activate a child's fantasy. Now let us try something different. Tie a handkerchief so that you have a figure with arms and legs; then make eyes with blobs of ink and perhaps a mouth with red ink as well; now a child must develop imagination to see the human form. This kind of thing works with tremendous living force on children, because it offers them the possibility of using fantasy.

Of course, we must do this ourselves first. But the possibility must be provided for children, and this must be done at the age when everything is play. This is why all the toys that do not stimulate fantasy in children are so damaging to them. As I said, today those "beautiful" dolls are somewhat outdated, because now we give monkeys or bears to children. Nor do such toys provide an opportunity for developing an imagination related to the human being. Suppose a child runs up to you, and you offer a bear for the child to cuddle. This sort of thing clearly shows how far our society is from being able to penetrate the depths of human nature. But it is remarkable how children, in a perfectly natural and artistic way, can form an imaginative picture of this inner side of human nature.

In the Waldorf school, we have shifted from the ordinary methods of teaching to what we may call "teaching through art." We never begin by teaching children to write; rather, we allow them paint as they draw, and draw as they paint. We could even say that we let them splash around, which involves the sometimes tiresome job of cleaning up the classroom afterward. Tomorrow, I will speak of how we lead from writing to reading. Apart from painting and drawing, however, we guide the children as far as possible into the realm of art by letting them practise modeling in their own ways, without suggesting that they should make anything except what they want to make out of their inner being. The results are remarkable. I will mention one example that shows how something very wonderful takes place in the case of older children.

At a relatively early age, for children between ten and eleven, a subject in our curriculum is the study of the human being. At this age, children learn how the bones are formed and built up, how they support one another, and so on. They learn this in an artistic way, not intellectually. After a few such lessons, the children have gained some perception of the structure of the human skeleton, the dynamics of the bones, and the nature of their interdependence. Then we move to the crafts room, where they model plastic forms, and we observe what they make. We see that they have learned something from their lessons about the bones. Not that the children imitate the forms of the bones; but from the way they now model the forms, we perceive the outer expression of an inner flexibility of soul. Before this, they have already advanced far enough to make various kinds of small receptacles; the children discover how to make bowls and similar things all by themselves. But what they create through the spontaneity of childhood before such lessons is very different from what they model afterward, provided they have truly experienced what was intended. To achieve this, however, our lessons on knowledge of the human being must be given in such a way that their essence enters the whole human being. Today, this has become difficult.

Those who have paid as many visits to art studios as I have, observing the way people paint and sculpt and carve, know very well that hardly any sculptor today works without a model; they need a human form in front of them before they can sculpt it. To the ancient Greek artists, this would have made no sense. Of course, they had learned the human form at the public games, but they truly experienced it inwardly. They knew, out of their inner feeling—a feeling they embodied without a model—the difference between an arm that is stretched out and an outstretched arm with the forefinger extended as well, and they embodied this in their works.

Today, when physiology is taught in the conventional way, models or drawings of the bones are placed side by side, the muscles are described one after another, and no impression is offered concerning their reciprocal relationship. At out school, when the children see a vertebra of the spinal column, they recognize its similarity to the skull, and they get a feeling for the metamorphosis of the bones. In this way, in a lively way they enter directly into the various human forms and thus feel an urge to express it artistically. Such experiences go right into life; they do not remain external.

It is my earnest wish and my duty as leader of the Waldorf school to eliminate from the classroom, whenever possible, everything of a scientific nature that is fixed, including textbooks written in a rigid scientific way. I value science—no one could value it more. Such studies may be pursued outside of school, if so desired, but I would become very upset if I saw a teacher standing before a class holding a book. When teaching, everything must come from within; this should be self-evident. How is botany taught today, for example? We have botany books based on a scientific view, but they do not belong in any classroom in which the children are between the change of teeth and puberty. The perception of what sort of literature a teacher needs must grow gradually from the living educational principles I will speak of here.

We are indeed concerned with the mental attitude of the teachers and whether they can relate to the world in soul, spirit, and body. If they possess a living relationship, there is much they can accomplish with children between the change of teeth and puberty, because, through this method, they can become the naturally accepted authority. The important thing is to get into and experience matters in a living way, bringing to life everything you have experienced in this way. This is the great, fundamental principle that must become the foundation of education today. Then one's connection with the class will arise automatically, along with the imponderable mood and feeling that needs to go with it.

Rudolf Steiner's answer to a question:

Question: Some adults seem to have remained at the imitative stage of childhood. Why does this happen?

Rudolf Steiner: At any stage of human development, it is possible to remain in a fixed state. If we describe the various stages of development, including the embryonic stage in today's survey and continuing through the change of teeth and on to puberty, we cover periods in which a fully developed human life can be formed. Recently, the general trend of anthroposophic development made it possible for lectures to address therapeutic, or curative, education, with particular reference to specific cases of children whose development was either retarded or in some way abnormal. We then took the step of showing certain cases that were being treated at Dr. Ita Wegman's clinic. Among these, there was a child who was almost a year old and about the average size for a child of that age. However, this child's physical body had remained at the embryonic stage of approximately seven or eight months. If you were to draw an outline of the child with only an indication of the limbs, which were somewhat more developed, and show the exact form of this little boy's head, then, looking closely at the drawing, you would not have the slightest idea that this boy was nearly a year old. You would think it the picture of an embryo, because this boy had, in many ways, retained an embryonic structure after his birth.

Every stage of life, including the embryonic, can be carried over into a later stage; the different phases of development, as they follow one another, are such that each new phase is a metamorphosis of the previous, with something new added. Consider exactly what I said about the natural religious devotion that children have toward their surroundings up to the change of teeth; you can see that this changes into the life of soul as well as a second attribute, the aesthetic, or artistic, stage. It happens with many children that the first stage is carried into the second, which then remains poorly developed. But this can go even further; the first stage of physical embodiment can be carried over into each of the others, so that attributes of the original stage appear in all the later stages. Even to superficial observation, it doesn't need to be very obvious that an earlier stage has been retained in a later one, unless it doesn't show up until particularly late in life. Nevertheless, it is a fact that earlier stages are carried into later ones.

Consider the same phenomenon in a lower kingdom of nature. A fully grown and developed plant usually has a root and a stalk with cotyledon leaves, followed by green leaves. These are then concentrated in the calyx, the petals, the stamen, the pistil, and so on. There are plants, however, that do not develop as far as the blossom, but remain at the stage of herbs and other plants in which the green leaves remain fixed, with merely rudimentary fruit. Notice, for example, how far the fern remains behind the buttercup. In a plant this does not indicate abnormality. Human beings, however, are of a species that forms a complete natural order. And it can happen that, throughout life, one remains at the imitative state or requires an authority figure. In life, we are dealing not only with people who remain at the imitative stage, but also with those who remain essentially at the stage that develops fully between the change of teeth and puberty. In fact, there are many such people, and for them this stage continues into later life. They cannot go much further, and the attributes that should develop in later years can do so only in a limited way. They remain at the stage where they look for the support of authority. If such people did not exist, there would be no tendency today to form sects and the like, because sectarian associations are based on the fact that their followers are not required to think; they leave the thinking to others and follow their leaders. In certain areas of life, however, people remain largely at the stage of authority. For instance, when it is a matter of forming a judgment about something scientific, people do not take the trouble to investigate it themselves, but ask for the conclusion of an expert or specialist who lectures at a universities. This is the principle of authority.

In the case of those who are ill, the principle of authority may be carried to extremes, though this may be justifiable. And in legal matters, for example, no one today would consider forming an independent judgment but seek the advice of a lawyer, who has the necessary knowledge. Here the perspective is that of a child of eight or nine; and the attorney is probably not much older. When a lawyer is asked a question, a lawbook is generally consulted, and once again we have an authority. So it is certainly true that each stage of life can enter a later one.

The Anthroposophical Society should really consist only of those who are outgrowing authority and who recognize only the principle of true insight. This is little understood by people outside the society, who continually assert that anthroposophy is based on authority. In fact, the exact opposite is true; the principle of authority must be outgrown through the kind of understanding and discernment fostered by anthroposophy. The important thing is to grasp every scrap of insight we can get hold of to pass through the various stages of life.

4 | The Three Stages of Childhood

July 20, 1924

As a result of yesterday's lecture, I was asked about our subject, and I would like to answer it here. The question is this: "In regard to the principle of imitation in a child's movements, I would like you to explain something. My grandfather died when my father was around a year and a half to two years old. Later, when he was about forty-five, my father visited one of my grandfather's friends, who was astonished at the similarity between my father's movements and gestures and those of my grandfather. What was the cause of this? Because of my grandfather's early death, it could hardly be a matter of imitation."

A man died when his son was a year and a half to two years old, and long afterward, when the son was forty-five, he heard from this friend, who was able to know that even as late as forty-five years old, he imitated, or rather, had the same gestures as his father.

Here we are dealing, of course, with matters in which one can do little more than provide certain guidelines, without any detailed explanations. Unfortunately, our lecture courses are short, and to cover this theme fully would require many lectures, perhaps six months or even a year. Many such questions are likely to arise, and it may be possible to answer them if they are presented. But I must point out that, because of our limited time, there will be a certain lack of clarity, which cannot be made clear unless it were possible to go into every detail fully. With reference to the question asked, I should like to offer the following remarks.

If we consider the first period of a child's life, between birth and the change of teeth, a child's organization works and develops in such a way that predispositions are incorporated into the organism. I described this yesterday as walking (including the general orientation of human beings), speaking, and thinking. And this is how events follow one another. Between the first and seventh year of life, children are organized so that they are concerned primarily with gesture; between around the seventh to fourteenth years, they are concerned with speech, as I explained yesterday; and, approximately, between the fourteenth and twenty-first years, they are organized so that they are concerned mainly with thinking. What thus appears in the course of twenty-one years is already taking shape as predispositions during the first period of life, between birth and the change of teeth.

During the first third of the first period of life, or during the first two and a third years of life, the assimilation of gestures takes place. This includes walking freely without support, so that the arms and the muscles of the face can move in an expressive way—that is, a general orientation and finding a living relationship to gestures and movements. The main development of children during this period is the development of gestures, which then continue to develop; but now something more intimate and inner is impressed into the speech organism. Even if a child has already spoken a few words, the experience of speech as predisposition does not occur before children are a little older than two and a half. The actual experience and feeling for speech is fully developed between the seventh and fourteenth year, but as predisposition it is present between two and a third and four and two thirds years. Of course, this must be taken as an average. After that, children develop a faculty for the beginning of the inner experience of thought. What develops and blossoms later, between fourteen and twenty-one, is already germinating between four and two thirds and seven years old. The formation of gestures continues, of course, throughout these years, but other faculties also come into play. Thus we see that, essentially, we must place the time of gestural development and formation back to the first two and a half years. What we gain during this time lies deepest. And this is only natural, since we can certainly imagine how fundamental the principle of imitation is during those first years of life.

If you consider all of this together, you will not be surprised by the events that led to this question. The grandfather died when the father was between one and a half and two years old—precisely the time when the formation of gesture is working most deeply. If the grandfather died then, the gestures the child imitated then made the deepest impression. This does not alter what may have been imitated later from others. So this particular case has extraordinary significance when considered in detail.

Yesterday we tried to describe how, as children develop during the second period of life, between the change of teeth and puberty, they experience everything expressed through speech, in which the natural authority of the teacher must play a role. The interaction between teacher and child must work in a pictorial, imaginative way. I pointed out how, at this age, we cannot approach children with moral precepts; rather, we can affect their moral character only by awakening feelings in them with pictures. In this way, the children take in images described by their teacher, who also acts as their model. The images work in such a way that goodness pleases them, and they develop a distaste for what is bad. Consequently, at the elementary school age, morality must be instilled through pictures by way of feelings.

I also explained that writing must be presented to children through images, and that the forms of letters must be developed through drawn paintings and painted drawings. Of all the arts, this must be cultivated first, since it leads children into culture. From an educational perspective, it is totally inappropriate to begin by introducing children to letter forms, which are alien to them; the fixed forms of letters as used today work on children like little demons.

When education is based on knowledge of the human being, children must learn to write before learning to read. If you wish to approach children of this age (immediately after the change of teeth), as much as possible you must approach the whole being of the children. When children are writing, it activates the whole upper body; the inner flexibility of children is different that it would be if only the head is busy learning the forms of letters. The liberated, independent faculties of the head cannot be used until a later age. Thus we can create a transition by allowing children to read what they have written, which makes an impression on them.

Because of this method of teaching at the Waldorf school, our children learn to read a bit later than others do, and they learn to write letters later than the children in other schools. One cannot really judge this fact, however, without a true understanding of human nature. Usually, people today have a limited perception and sense of the human being and do not notice how harmful it is for general human development when children learn reading and writing too early; these things are too far removed from them. Certainly the children whose proficiency in these arts is attained somewhat later than others will not experience any lack in their capacity to read and write. On the other hand, those who learn to read and write too early will certainly suffer in this respect. Education based on a knowledge of the human being must, from the very beginning, arise from this ability to "read" human evolution; by understanding the conditions of life, we can help children develop their own nature. This is the *only* way toward a truly healthy education.

To gain deeper understanding, we must penetrate the human being. First, the human being consists of a physical body, which is developed most intensively during the first period of life. The main development during the second period is the higher and finer body, the ether body. It is very important that, when we study the human being, we do so in a truly scientific way, and we must invoke a degree of courage equal to that shown in other areas of modern science.

A substance that shows a certain degree of warmth can be brought to a state in which that warmth, which has been bound up with substance, is freed. It is liberated and becomes "free" warmth. In the case of mineral substances, we have the courage to speak scientifically when we say that there is "bound" warmth and "free" warmth. We must have the same courage when we study the world as a whole. If we have the courage, the following reveals itself to us in regard to the human being.

Where are the forces of the ether body during the first period of life? They are bound up with the physical body and are active in its nourishment and growth. In this first period, children are different from what they become later. All the forces of the ether body are initially bound up with the physical body. At the end of the first period, they are freed to some extent, just as warmth is freed from a substance with which it had been bound. What happens now? After the change of teeth, only part of the ether body is active in the forces of growth and nourishment; the part that has been liberated now carries on the more intensive development of memory and soul qualities. Because it is a fact, we must learn to speak of the soul as "bound" during the first seven years of life, and to speak of the soul as "liberated" after the seventh year. What we use as soul forces during the second seven-year period of life is, during the first seven years, imperceptibly bound up with the physical body, when nothing psychic can be free of the body. We can gain knowledge of how the soul works during that first seven years by observing the body. Only after the change of teeth can we directly approach what is purely of a soul nature.

This way of viewing matters leads directly from the physical to the psychological. Consider the myriad approaches to psychology today. They are based on speculation, pure and simple. People think matters over and discover that, on the one hand, we have a soul and, on the other, a body. We must ask: Does the body give rise to and work on the soul, or does it work in the opposite direction? If they do not manage to get any further either way, people discover something extraordinarily bizarre:

"psychophysical parallelism," the notion that both manifestations run parallel. As a result, no explanation is given for the interaction between them; one speaks only of *parallelism*. This indicates that nothing is known through experience about these matters. Experience leads one to say that, during the first seven years of life in children, one perceives the soul working in the body. The way this works must be learned through observation, not merely through speculation. Spiritual science, as a way of knowledge, completely rejects speculation and always proceeds from experience—physical *and* spiritual experience, of course.

So, during the second period of life between the change of teeth and puberty, the human ether body is our main concern in education. Above all, both teacher and child need the forces at work in the ether body, because they release the child's feeling life, not judgment and thought. Deeply embedded in the nature of children between the change of teeth and puberty is the third member of the human being, the astral body, which bears all feelings and sensations. During this period, the astral body is still deeply embedded in the ether body. Thus, because the ether body has now become relatively free, it is our task to develop it so that it can follow its own tendencies, which are helped by education, not hindered. When can it be helped? This happens when we teach children through pictures, in the broadest sense; everything we wish them to absorb we build imaginatively and in images. The ether body is the body of formative forces; it models the wonderful forms of the organs—the heart, lungs, liver, and so on. The physical body, which we inherit, acts only as a model; after the first seven years—after the change of teeth—it is laid aside, and a second physical body is formed by the etheric body. This is why, at this age, our educational methods must be adapted to the formative forces of the ether body.

We must proceed in such a way that children gradually learn to find their orientation in the world. I have already said that I find it very repugnant when I see a scientific textbook that has been brought to school for the purpose of teaching along those lines. Today's science, which I acknowledge fully, has deviated in many ways from a worldview that truly accords with nature. Now let's just ask ourselves a question—bearing in mind that, as our discussion proceeds, other matters may need to be added—What is the approximate age when we can begin to teach children about the plant world?

We teach children by means of pictures, and they learn to write through painting and drawing; indeed, it is never too early to introduce children to the arts, since all our teaching must be imbued with a feeling for art. In the same way, we must also keep this in mind: Just as the ether body is inseparable from the human formative and pictorial aspects, the astral body, which underlies the life of feelings and sensations, tends toward the musical nature of a person. So what do we look for when observing children? Because the astral body is embedded in the physical and etheric bodies of children between the change of teeth and puberty, if the soul life is healthy it is also deeply musical. Every healthy child is profoundly musical. To invoke this musicality, we need only call on the children's own natural liveliness and sense of movement. Artistic teaching, from the very beginning of school life, should thus employ both the visual arts and music. We should never emphasize abstraction; an artistic approach is most important, and children must be led to comprehend the world out of the artistic.

This must not be done too late or too early. We must be aware of a very important stage in the development of children between the ages of nine and ten. Those who look with the eyes of a teacher see this in every child. Although they do not usually express it in so many words, a time comes when children reveal through their behavior that they have a question or several questions that betray an inner crisis. This is an extremely delicate experience in children, and we need an exceptionally delicate sense for such things to perceive it; it is present and can be observed. At this age, children learn intuitively to differentiate themselves from the surrounding world. Before this age, the "I" and the outer world interpenetrate each other, and so we can tell the children stories about animals, plants, and rocks whose actions make them seem human. Indeed, this is the ideal approach, because we should appeal to their pictorial, imaginative sense, and we do this by speaking this way about the kingdoms of nature. Between ten and eleven, however, children learn to say "I" in self-awareness. They learn this earlier, of course, but now they do it consciously. Once their consciousness is no longer merged with the outer world, and once they have learned to distinguish themselves from it, we can begin to help children understand the plant world with feeling, but without immediately renouncing the element of image and imagination.

Today we are used to looking at one plant next to another; we learn their names and related information, and we do this as though a plant were there independently. But when we study plants in this way, it is like pulling out a hair, forgetting that it was on your head, and examining it as though you can understand its nature and life-conditions without considering that it grew from your head. The hair has meaning only when we consider the fact that it grew on a head; it cannot be studied in isolation. It is the same for a plant. We cannot pull it up and study it separately; we must consider the earth as an organism to which the plant belongs. This is what it is. Plants belong to the entire growth of the earth, just as a hair belongs to the head. Plants can never be studied in isolation, but only in relation to the whole nature of the earth. The earth and the world of plants belong together.

Suppose you had a herbaceous plant, an annual, growing from its roots, shooting up into a stalk, leaves, and flowers, and developing the fruit that is planted again the following year. Then you have the earth in which the plant grows. Now think of a tree. A tree lives longer; it is not an annual. It develops a mineralized bark around itself, from which pieces can be broken off. In reality, what sort of process is this? If you were to build up the surrounding earth and its inherent forces around a plant, more or less covering it with earth, then you would recreate this process synthetically in an outer, mechanical way. Nature does the same thing, however, by wrapping the tree with the bark; but in this case it is not made completely of earth. The bark forms a kind of earth mound that piles itself up around the tree. When we look at a growing tree, we see the earth flourishing and growing. This is why the earth that surrounds the root of a plant must be considered a part of it; the soil belongs to a plant.

If you have learned to observe such things and happen to travel in an area where you see many plants with yellow flowers, you will immediately try to see the sort of soil they grow in. In particular, wherever we see many yellow flowers, for instance, we are likely to find somewhat reddish soil. You will never be able to think about the plant without considering the earth in which it grows; they go together. We should quickly become accustomed to this fact; otherwise, we destroy our sense for reality.

I was deeply impressed recently during an agricultural course I gave at the request of some farmers.* At the end of the lecture course, a farmer said, "Everyone today knows that our vegetables are dying out and becoming decadent with alarming speed." Why is this? It is because people no longer understand, as peasants used to, that earth and plants are connected and must be considered in this way. If we want to nurture our vegetables so that they flourish again, we must understand how to treat them correctly; in other words, we must give them the right kind of manure. We must make it possible for the earth to live properly in the environment of the plant roots. Today, because agricultural methods of cultivation have failed, we need a new agricultural impulse based on spiritual science. This will enable us to use manure in such a way that plant growth does not degenerate. Those who are as old as I am know what European potatoes looked like fifty years ago compared to the way they look today. Today, we see more than just a decline of Western culture; this decline also penetrates deeply into the kingdoms of nature, including agriculture.

It really amounts to this: Our sense of the connection between plants and their environment should not be lost. On school outings and similar occasions, plants should

---

* See *Spiritual Foundations for the Renewal of Agriculture* (8 lectures, Koberwitz, Silesia, June 7–16, 1924), Kimberton, PA: Bio-Dynamic Farming and Gardening Association, 1993.

not be pulled up, placed in specimen containers, and brought to the classroom in the belief that we accomplish something by doing this. Uprooted plants cannot exist by themselves. People today indulge completely false ideas. For example, they view a piece of chalk and a flower as having the same sort of reality. But this is nonsense. A mineral object can exist in itself; this is a fact. So people believe that the plant should also have an independent existence; but this is impossible, since it ceases to be a plant once it is pulled from the ground. It maintains its earthly existence only while it is attached to something other than itself; and that "other" has existence only insofar as it is part of the whole earth. We must study phenomena within the whole, not tear them out of it.

Almost all knowledge based on observation is filled with unrealities of this kind. This is why natural science has become so abstract, though this is partially justified, as it is for the theory of relativity. But those who can think realistically do not allow abstract concepts to run on and on without noticing the point where they cease to have any relationship to reality. That would be painful. Naturally, you could use the principles of acoustics and say: When I make a sound, the sound travels at a certain speed. Wherever I hear a sound, I can calculate the exact time it took to reach me. If I move in the same direction in which the sound travels—regardless of my speed—I will hear it later. And if I were traveling faster than the speed of sound, I would not hear it at all. But by moving toward the sound, I hear it earlier. The theory of relativity is definitely reasonable, but according to this principle, we could also say that, if I were to move toward the sound more quickly than the speed of sound, I would go beyond it and hear the sound before it is made.

This fact should be obvious to anyone who can think realistically. Such a person also knows that it is absolutely logical and wonderfully thought out to say that if a clock (to use the well-known comparison of Einstein) is thrown at the speed of light into universal space and returns, it will not have changed at all. This can be thought through in a wonderful way. But those who think realistically must ask: What will the clock look like on its return? Realistic thinking does not separate the thinking from the reality, but always remains in the realm of reality.

This is the essential characteristic of spiritual science; it requires more than mere logic; it approaches matters in accordance with reality. This is why people today—who carry abstractions to the point of splitting hairs—accuse anthroposophists of being abstract, simply because our way of thinking always looks for absolute truth and never loses its connection with reality, which must include an understanding of spiritual reality. This is why it is possible to see how unnatural it is to associate botany with specimens in a container.

When we introduce children to botany, therefore, it is important to consider the earth's face, dealing with the soil and the growing plants together so that children will never think of plants as detached and separate. This can be unpleasant for teachers who would simply like to bring the usual botany books to class, give them a quick glance during lessons, and then act as though they understand it all. I already said that there are no suitable textbooks on botany these days. And this sort of teaching assumes another aspect once we understand the effect of imponderables, and when we consider that the subconscious works even more strongly in children than it does in older people. The subconscious is very clever, and those who are able to perceive children's spiritual life know this: when students are faced with a teacher who walks around the class with notes while trying to convey the substance of these notes, the children always wonder why they should learn such information; after all, the teacher doesn't even know it. This becomes a tremendous disturbance to the lessons, because those feelings arise from the subconscious; nothing can be expected of a class taught by a teacher using notes.

We must always look at the spiritual aspect of matters. This is especially true when we are developing an art of education, since this is how we give children a sense of standing firmly and safely in the world. They gradually come to understand that the earth is an organism—and, in fact, this is what it is. When soil begins to lose its vitality, we must help it by using manure in the right way. For example, it is not true that water in the air is the same as water in the earth. The water below has a certain vitality; the water above loses that vitality, which it regains only as it descends. These are facts and absolutely real. If we fail to understand them, we cannot unite with the world in a real way. This then is what I wished to say in regard to teaching about the plant world.

Now we come to the animal world, and we cannot view animals as belonging to the earth in the same way. The mere fact that the animals can move about makes this obvious; in this sense, they are independent. But when we compare animals with humankind, we find something characteristic in their formation. This was always indicated in the older instinctive science, the effects of which still existed at the beginning of the ninth century. Because of the way modern people look at things, however, when they read the views of natural philosophers who, following old traditions, considered the animal world's relationship to the world of humankind, their ideas seem foolish. I realize, for example, that people in a study group can hardly contain their laughter when they read this from the natural philosopher Oken: "The human tongue is a cuttlefish."[*] What could he have meant by this? In fact, this statement from Oken can no longer be considered correct, but it contains an underlying principle that we must take into account.

When we observe the various animal forms, from the tiniest protozoa to the most fully developed apes, we find that they all represent some part of the human being—a human organ or an organic system—that has developed in a one-sided way. You don't need to look at these things in a very deep way. Just imagine that the human forehead enormously withdrawn; the jaw jutting out; the eyes looking upward instead of toward the front; the teeth and their whole organization formed in a one-sided way. By imagining such extreme developments you can picture a great variety of mammals. By eliminating one thing or another in the human form, you can change it into an ox, a sheep, and so on.

When you can consider the inner organs—for example, those related to reproduction—you enter the area of the lower animals. The human being is a synthesis or assembly of individual animal forms that become softer and

---

[*] Lorenz Oken (1779–1851), the German transcendental naturalist and philosopher, wrote numerous natural-philosophical and natural-historical works. Between 1816 to 1848, as a professor in Jena, Oken published the periodical *Isis*, a forum for all academic subjects (except theology and law). The periodical gave rise to controversy because of the political views expressed. Goethe, who had a personal enmity toward Oken, and others called for a ban on the periodical, and eventually both the magazine and Oken were banned from Jena.

gentler when united. The human being is made up of all the animals, formed into a harmonious structure. Thus, when I look for the original forms that merge in the human being, I find the whole animal world. The human being is a condensation of the whole animal world.

This view restores our soul's proper relationship to the animal world. It has been forgotten, but it is nevertheless the correct view, and, because it is essential to the principles of evolution, it must be restored to life. We show children how the plant belongs to the earth; then when they are about eleven years old, insofar as this is possible today, we must begin to consider the animal world. We do this in such a way that we see the various animal forms in the human being. Consider the effect this has on children's relationship to animals and plants. Plants go into the earth and unite with it; animals become one with the human being. This provides a basis for a real relationship to the world; it gives humankind a real relationship to the world. This can always be brought to children in connection with the subject matter. If this is presented to children in an artistic and living way, and if it corresponds to the capacity of their inner being, we give them the living forces they need to establish a relationship to life. On the other hand, it is easy to destroy that relationship by failing to look deeply at the whole human being.

What, in fact, is the ether body? If it were possible to lift it out of the physical body and imbue it in such a way that its form became visible, there could be no greater work. The human ether body, by its own nature and through what we create within it, is simultaneously a work of art and the artist. When we introduce the formative element into the children's artwork, we allow them to sculpt with the freedom I described yesterday; what we bring them is deeply related to the ether body. This enables children to take hold of their inner being and thus, as human beings, claim their proper relationship to the world.

By introducing children to music, we form the astral body. But when we put two things together, taking the formative into movement, and when we perform movements that are formative, we have eurythmy, which follows exactly the relationship between the ether and astral bodies in children. So now the children learn eurythmy, or speech revealed in formed gestures, just as they learned quite naturally to speak in their earlier years. Healthy children have no difficulty learning eurythmy, because in eurythmy they simply express their own being; they have the impulses to express their own being. This is why, in addition to gymnastics, eurythmy is incorporated into the curriculum as a required subject, from the first years through the highest grades.

You see, eurythmy arose from the whole human being—the physical, etheric, and astral bodies; it can be studied only by means of spiritual scientific knowledge of the human being. Today, gymnastics are directed physiologically toward the body in a lopsided way; because physiology cannot do otherwise, it introduces certain principles based on life-giving processes. Through gymnastics, however, we do not educate the whole human being, but only one aspect. This is not said to imply anything against gymnastics, but today the importance of gymnastics is overrated. Thus, in today's education, eurythmy should go hand in hand with gymnastics.

I would not go so far as one well-known physiologist did. He happened to be in the audience when I spoke on eurythmy. I said that, in terms of education, gymnastics are overrated today, and that a form of gymnastics calling on the forces of soul and spirit—as practiced in eurythmy along with the study of eurythmy as an art—must be introduced in addition to the usual gymnastics. At the end of my lecture, the famous physiologist approached me and said, "Do you mean to tell me that gymnastics may be a valid means of education because physiologists say it is so? As a physiologist, I must tell you that gymnastic education is nothing less than barbaric." You would very surprised if I told you the name of that physiologist. Today, these things have become obvious to those who have some authority, and we must be careful not to advocate fanatically without full knowledge of everything involved. To become a fanatic over certain things is completely out of place in the art of education, because we are dealing with many different aspects of life.

When we approach other subjects that children must be taught, and when we do so from the various views we have considered, we first come to the years when children can absorb only images through feelings. For example, history and geography must be taught in this way. History must be described in images; we paint and sculpt with words, which develops children's minds. During the first two stages of the second period of life, there is one thing, above all, to which children do not relate; we could call this the idea of causation. Before the seventh year, children should certainly not attend school.* The time from seven to just past nine years of age is the first subdivision of the second main period of life; from just past nine to just before twelve years old is the second stage;

---

* Kindergarten, in this case, is not considered to be school as such.

and from eleven years eight months until around fourteen is the third stage.

During the first stage of this second period of life, children are organized so that they respond to images in a direct way. Therefore, we must speak as we would in fairytales, because everything must remain undifferentiated from the children's own nature. Plants must speak to one another; minerals must speak together; plants must kiss one another and have fathers and mothers. Around nine years and four months, the self has been characterized—the I begins to differentiate itself from the outer world. Now we can take a more realistic approach when teaching about plants and animals. During the first years of life, however, history must always be approached in a fairytale and mythical attitude. In the second division of this longer period—from about nine years and four months until eleven years and eight months, we must speak in images. It is only as they approach the age of twelve that we may introduce children to causation; only then can we go into to abstract concepts, allowing cause and effect to come into play. Before this, the idea of cause and effect is beyond the reach of children, just as colors are to those who are color blind; as educators, we frequently have no idea how useless it is to speak to children about cause and effect. It is only after children reach the age of twelve that we can speak to them about things that are taken for granted when viewed from today's scientific perspective.

It is thus essential that we wait until about the twelfth year before dealing with anything related to the inorganic, since this means getting into the concept of causation. Also, when teaching history, we must wait until about this age before going from a pictorial presentation to one that involves cause and effect, when we look for the causes behind historical events. Before this, we should concern ourselves only with what we can present to children as life imbued with soul.

People are very strange indeed. For instance, through the development of culture, a concept has arisen that we call "animism." It is said that if a child bumps into a table, the table is seen to be alive, and the child strikes back at it. Children "dream" a soul into the table, and it is believed that primitive people did the same. The idea is that something very complex occurs in the souls of children. They supposedly think that the table is actually alive with soul, and this is why they hit back when they bump into it. This is fantastic. On the contrary, those who study cultural history are the ones who actually do the ensouling, since they ensoul children with this imaginative capacity. But children's soul qualities are far more deeply embedded in the physical body than they are later on, when they are freed. When a child bumps into a table, a reflex occurs without any thought that the table is alive. It is a purely reflexive movement of will, since children do not yet differentiate themselves from the outer world.

This differentiation does not appear until around the twelfth year, when healthy children can grasp the concept of causation. If this concept is presented to children too early—especially in superficial, external ways— terrible conditions are set up for their development. It's all very well to say that we should make sure everything is perfectly clear to a child. Calculators exist in which little balls are pushed around to make the mathematical operations visible. The next thing we may expect is that those with such an attitude will make moral concepts outwardly visible by using some kind of machine that pushes something around to show good and evil, just as calculators allow us to see that $5 + 7 = 12$. There are undoubtedly areas of life in which things cannot be made visible and are nevertheless absorbed by children in ways that are not obvious at all; and it is a big mistake when we try to make them so. Hence, it is very wrong to attempt, as is often done in textbooks, to make something visible that, by its very nature, cannot be treated in that way. People frequently become trivial in this way.

During the years between the change of teeth and puberty, we are concerned not just with the obvious, because when we consider the whole of human life something else also becomes obvious. At the age of eight, I absorb some concept; I do not yet understand it fully—in fact, I don't understand its abstract meaning at all. I am not yet constituted in a way that makes this possible. So why do I take in such a concept at all? It is because my teacher is speaking; my teacher's authority is a given, and it works on me. These days, however, we are not supposed to do this; children are supposed to be shown only what is visible and obvious.

Consider children who are taught everything in this way. Their experiences do not grow with them, because this method treats them as a beings who do not grow. But we should not awaken ideas in children if those ideas are unable to grow with them; this is like making a pair of shoes for a three-year-old and expecting that child to wear them at the age of twelve. Everything in human beings grows, including the power of comprehension; consequently, concepts must be able to grow as well. We must therefore make sure we bring living concepts to children, but we cannot do this unless children have a living relationship to the teacher's authority. And this cannot be accomplished by abstract, pedantic teachers who stand in front of children and give them concepts that are still completely alien to them.

Imagine two children. One has been taught in such a way that, even at the age of forty-five, she continues to take in concepts and explain them as she did at the age of eight. The concept has not grown with the child; she paid careful attention to it all, and at forty-five she still explains it in the same way. Now consider the second child, who has been educated in a living way. He no longer wears the same size shoes that he did when he was eight, and likewise, at a later age, he no longer carries around the same concepts that he learned when he was eight. On the contrary—those concepts have expanded and changed radically. And all of this affects the physical body. If we look at these two people in relation to their physical fitness, we find that the first person will have sclerosis by the age of forty-five, whereas the second has remained more flexible. How much do you think human beings differ? Someplace in Europe, there were two philosophy professors. One was famous for his Greek philosophy; the other was an old adherent of the Hegelian school, in which people were still used to taking in living concepts, even after the age of twenty. Both lectured at the same university. At seventy, the first professor decided to exercise his right to retire, since he felt that he could not continue. The second—the Hegelian professor—was ninety-one when he said, "I cannot understand why that young fellow is settling down to retirement already." The conceptual life of this second professor had remained flexible. And for this very reason, people criticized and accused him of being inconsistent. The other man was consistent, but he suffered from sclerosis.

There is a complete unity in children between spirit and body, and we cannot approach them correctly unless we consider this. Today, people who do not sympathize with materialistic views will say that materialism is bad. Why is that? Many say it is bad because it does not understand spirit. But this is not the worst thing about it because, little by little, people will become aware of this lack and come to recognize spirit because of an urge to understand it. The worst thing about materialism is that it does not understand matter. Look into this for yourselves; you can see what has happened to knowledge of the living forces in the human lung, liver, and so on because of materialism. Nothing is known about how these things function. Something is left out of the lung and liver; it may be prepared and examined, but modern scientific methods cannot learn anything about the spirit that functions actively in human organs. Such knowledge can be learned only through spiritual science. Matter reveals its nature only when studied from the perspective of spiritual science.

Materialism has become sick, mostly because materialists understand nothing about matter. They want to limit themselves to matter, but they cannot reach any real knowledge of what matter is. In saying this, I do not mean theorized matter, in which a certain number of atoms supposedly dance around a central nucleus: such things are not very difficult to construct. In the earlier days of the Theosophical Society, some theosophists constructed a whole system based on atoms and molecules; but it was just theory. Now we have to approach reality again. If we actually do this, we become uncomfortable when we are expected to comprehend a concept entirely void of reality. It would be painful if someone were to

promote a theory such as this one, for example: Fundamentally it is the same thing whether you drive your car
to town or the car remains immobile and the town comes
to you. Certainly, such things are justified when viewed
from a certain perspective. But they impoverish the
whole soul life when extended as they are today by those
who hold completely abstract opinions.

Those who have a sense for these things experience real
pain when confronted by what people think today, and
this works destructively on teaching methods as well. For
example, I see the tendencies of certain methods that are
applied to little kindergarten children. They are given the
usual cutout letters and then asked to pick them out of a
pile and assemble them into words. By busying children
this way at such an early age, we bring them things with
which they have absolutely no connection. When this
happens to them, it's as if we were to say, I was once a
person with muscles, skin, and such, but now I am only a
skeleton. This is the way it is today; because of the influence of our propensity for abstractions in spiritual life of
humankind, one suddenly sees oneself as a skeleton. We
cannot educate children with such a view—with a bare
skeleton of reality.

This is the main reason I wanted to show you today
how crucial it is that teachers approach life in a true and
living way.

5 | Teachers' Conferences in Waldorf Schools

July 21, 1924

$\mathcal{A}$t this point in our educational studies, I would like to introduce some remarks about the arrangements that were made in the Waldorf school. This was done to facilitate and put into practice principles I have already spoken of and will discuss further in the following lectures.

Emil Molt

The Waldorf school in Stuttgart was begun in 1919 through the initiative of Emil Molt.* Its purpose was to carry out the principles of education based on anthroposophy. This was made possible because the direction and leadership of the school was entrusted to

---

* Emil Molt (1876–1939) was the head of the Waldorf Astoria Cigarette Company in Stuttgart. His confidence in Rudolf Steiner's educational ideas led him to begin a school based on those principles for the children of his workers.

me. Therefore, when I describe this school's organization, it can also serve as an example of how to realize these basic educational principles discussed here.

First, I would like to make it clear that the soul of all teaching and education in a Waldorf school is the teachers' conference. The "college of teachers" holds these conferences regularly, and I attend them whenever I can be in Stuttgart. They deal not only with external matters of school organization—creating schedules, forming classes, and so on; they also deal in a deep, far-reaching way with everything that affects the life and soul of the school. Matters are arranged to advance the school's goals—that is, education based on knowledge of the human being. This, of course, means that such knowledge must be applied to each individual child; time must be devoted to observing the psyche of each child. This is essential and must be considered in concrete detail when establishing the educational plan as a whole. In teachers' conferences, individual children are discussed in such a way that the teachers try to comprehend human nature as it relates to each child. You can certainly imagine that we have to deal with children of all levels and kinds, having various childlike talents and soul qualities. We are faced with just about every kind of child, from those we must consider poorly endowed, both psychologically and physically, to those (and let us hope life confirms this) who are gifted to the point of genius.

If we wish to observe children, in their true being, we must acquire a psychological faculty of perception. This sort of perception includes not just a superficial kind of ability to observe individual children, but, above all, the ability to appraise their capacities correctly. Just consider this: We may have a child in class who seems to be extraordinarily gifted in learning to read and write, or perhaps gifted at learning arithmetic or languages. It would be superficial, however, to steadfastly hold an opinion that this child is gifted because of an ability to easily learn languages or arithmetic. During childhood— say around seven to nine years old—a child's ease of learning may indicate that, later on, he or she will develop genius; but it can just as well indicate that, sooner or later, the child will become neurotic or in some way succumb to poor health. Once we have gained an understanding of the human being, we realize that a person consists of more than a perceptible physical body; there is also an ether body, which is the source of growth and nourishing forces, whereby children grow. We recognize that the human being also has an astral body, whose laws have nothing to do with physical manifestation but, on the contrary, work destructively on the physical, destroying it to make room for spirit. Furthermore, we recognize the presence of an I being connected to a person. Thus, we have three beings: ether body, astral body, I being, all of which we must acknowledge in addition to the perceptible physical body. In this way, we are able to form an idea of the complexity of human beings, and how each member of a human being might lead to a talent—or lack of talent—in any area. It can also reveal a false talent that is, in fact, transient and pathological. You must develop an understanding of whether a talent tends to be healthy or unhealthy.

As educators, if, you show the necessary love, devotion, and selflessness, and if you understand the human being as discussed in these lectures, then something very definite arises. By living with the children, you will become increasingly wise (do not misunderstand this word; it is not used in the sense of pride). You discover for yourself how to assess various capacities or achievements of the children. You quickly learn to penetrate a child's nature in a living way.

I realize that many people will say that if the human being, in addition to a physical body, consists of suprasensory members—ether, astral, and I organizations—it follows that teachers must be clairvoyant and able to perceive those suprasensory aspects of human nature. This, however, is not the case. Everything perceived through imagination, inspiration, and intuition (as described in my books) can be examined and assessed by simply observing the physical organization of a child, because it is always expressed in the physical body.

Consequently, for educators whose teaching is truly loving and based on a thorough knowledge of the human being, it is possible to speak of specific cases in a particular way. For example, the physical body may indicate hardening or stiffening, thus hindering a child from developing latent faculties that are present spiritually. Or, a child of about seven or eight might display certain attributes and surprise us by being able to learn something at a very early age; but we can see that the physical body is too soft and has a tendency to become fat later on. If the physical body is too soft—if, as it were, the fluid element weighs too much in relation to the solid element, this tendency leads the soul and spirit to make themselves felt too soon, and thus we are confronted by a precocious child. In such cases, as the physical body develops, this precocious quality is pushed back again, so that under certain conditions everything may change, and the child's whole of life may not only be average, but even below average. In other words, we must consider the fact that external observation of a child must be accompanied by inner perception; it means nothing at all to speak only of the presence or lack of faculties.

What I am saying can be confirmed by studying the biographies of the many kinds of people. By following the spiritual development of humankind, we could cite many distinguished individuals who accomplished great things later on in life, but were considered virtually without talent and incompetent as schoolchildren. We encounter some very remarkable examples in this connection. For example, there is a poet who, around the age of eighteen to twenty, was thought to be so ungifted by his educators that, for this reason, they advised him not to attempt a higher education. But he was not put off; he continued his studies, and before long, he was appointed inspector of the very schools that he was advised not to attend. And there was the Austrian poet, Robert Hamerling (1830–1889), who studied to become a secondary school teacher. In his examinations, he received excellent grades in Greek and Latin; on the other hand, he failed the test for teaching German, because his essays were considered inadequate. Nevertheless, he became a well-known poet.

We have found it necessary to separate some children from the others, permanently or for a brief time, because they are mentally slow and disturb the classes owing to their inability to understand. They are placed together in a special class for children of limited capacity. This class is taught by the man who has spoken to you here, Dr. Schubert, whose very special qualities make him a born leader of such a class.[*] Indeed, this task calls for special gifts.

---

[*] Dr. Karl Schubert (1881–1949) led the so-called auxiliary class of the Stuttgart Waldorf school.

Above all, it requires a gift for being able to penetrate into qualities of soul that are "imprisoned" within the physical and have difficulty freeing themselves. Little by little, however, they must be liberated. Here we again approach the borders of physical illness, where abnormal psychology impinges on the physically abnormal. It is possible to shift this boundary; it is certainly not fixed. In fact, it is helpful to look behind every so-called psychological abnormality and find what is unhealthy in the physical organism. In the truest sense of the word, there are no mental illnesses; they are the result of a disruption in the release of spirit from the physical.

In Germany today, we not only have the problem that nearly all schoolchildren are malnourished, but they have suffered the effects of undernourishment for years. So we are concerned with the fact that, by observing both the soul and physical body, we can begin to understand their essential unity. People find it difficult to understand that this is essential to education. One day a man visited the Waldorf school. He had considerable understanding and was directly engaged in school matters. For days, I showed him around personally, and he seemed interested in everything. And since our education is based on knowledge of the human being, we spoke mostly about the children instead of abstract educational principles. But after I had told him all I could about one child or another, he finally said, "This is all very well and good, but the teachers would all need medical degrees." To which I replied, "That's not necessary, but they should certainly have some medical knowledge, given all that the teachers need to know for their educational work."

Where will we be if, for some reason, it is said that we cannot provide for this, or that the teachers cannot learn it? We must provide for what is required and the teachers must learn what is needed. This is the only possible perspective. We can best study the "normal" capacities developed by every human being by observing pathological conditions. If you have come to understand a sick organism from various perspectives, then you have built a foundation for understanding a soul endowed with genius. I am not advocating the view of a Lombroso [an Italian criminologist] or someone holding similar views; this is not the case. I do not assert that genius is always a condition of sickness, but we do in fact come to understand the soul by understanding the sick body of a child. By studying the difficulties of soul and spirit that manifest outwardly in a sick body, we can come to understand how the soul takes hold of the organism when it needs to express something in particular.

Thus education encounters not only mild pathological conditions—such as those present in children of limited capacity—but it also encounters pathologies in the broadest sense. This is the reason why we introduced medical treatment for the children in our school. But we do not have a doctor who practices only medicine and remains outside the area of education; our school doctor, Dr. Kolisko, is also a class teacher.* He is completely within the school as a teacher; he is familiar with all the children, so he is in a position to understand the source of pathological symptoms that appear in the children. This is completely different from what is possible for school doctors who visit a school at specific times and assess the children's health after cursory observation. Aside from this, however, in the teachers' conferences there is no

---

* Eugen Kolisko, M.D. (1893–1939), teacher and school physician at the Waldorf school in Stuttgart.

hard and fast line between soul and body when a particular child is considered. The natural outcome of this is that the teachers must gradually come to understand the whole human being, so that they are equally interested in all the details of physical and mental health.

This is our goal in the school. The teachers should all have a deep interest in, and pay great attention to, the whole human being. So it follows that our teachers are not specialized in the ordinary sense. Essentially, the important thing is not that a history teacher has mastered the subject of history; instead, teachers should have the kind of personality that affects the children as we have described. The teachers need to be aware of how the children are developing under their care.

I myself had to teach from my fifteenth year on, just to make a living. I had to give private lessons, and so I gained practical experience in teaching. For example, when I was very young—just twenty-one—I took responsibility for the education of a family of four boys, and I became a resident in the family's home. At the time, one of the boys was eleven years old and obviously hydrocephalic. He had peculiar habits; he disliked eating at the table. He would leave the dining room and go into the kitchen, where there were containers for trash and food scraps. There, he ate potato peels and the other waste. At eleven years, he was still almost completely ignorant.

Earlier, as part of his instruction and in the hope that he could be received into a class, he was allowed to attempt a primary school entrance examination. When he handed in the examination results, however, the exercise book contained only one large hole, where he had erased something. He had accomplished nothing else at all, and he was eleven years old. The parents were very upset. They were part of the cultured upper middle class, and people commented on the boy's abnormality. Of course, when such things are said, people tend to feel a bias against the child. The common opinion was that he should learn a trade, since he was incapable of anything else.

I came into the family, but no one really understood me when I told them what I was prepared to do. I told them that, if I am given complete responsibility for the boy, I can promise only that I will try to evoke what is in the boy. Nobody understood this except his mother, who had an instinctive sense of perception, and their excellent family doctor. It was that doctor who later founded psychoanalysis, along with Dr. Freud—although, once it became decadent, he severed his connection with psychoanalysis. I was able to talk with that man, and our conversations led to the decision that I would be entrusted with the boy's education and training.

Within eighteen months, his head had become noticeably smaller, and the boy advanced enough to enter secondary school. I helped him further during his schooling, because he needed extra help. But after eighteen months, he was accepted as a secondary school student. Certainly, he had to be educated in such a way that sometimes I needed an hour and a half just to prepare what I wanted him to learn in fifteen minutes. It was necessary to teach him with great economy, never spending more time than absolutely necessary on any given subject. It was also a matter of arranging the day's schedule with great precision—a certain amount of time for music, for gymnastics, for going for a walk, and so on. If the boy is educated in this way, I told myself, then it will be possible to draw out his latent capacities. There were times when things went badly with such efforts. He became pale. Except for his mother and the family doctor, everyone said that I was ruining the boy's health. I replied that, of course, I would be unable to continue with his education if there was any interference. Things had be allowed to continue according to our agreement. And so it went.

The boy finished secondary school, continued his studies, and became a doctor. He did die an early death, but this was for the simple reason that he was called to serve as a doctor during the World War. There, he caught an infection and died of the ensuing illness. Nevertheless, he carried out his duties as a medical doctor in an admirable way. I present this example only to show you how important it is in education to view matters as a whole. It also shows how, through a specific program of education, it is even possible, week by week, to reduce a hydrocephalic condition.

Now you might say that, of course, something like this can happen in the case of private tutoring. But it can just as well happen in a relatively large class. Anyone who enters lovingly into what is presented here as the knowledge of the human being can quickly acquire the ability to observe each child with the necessary attention. One can do this even in a large class. In this case, however, the psychological perception I have described is especially important. But such perception is not easily acquired by those who go through the world as isolated individuals with absolutely no interest in others. I can truly say that I am indebted to the fact that I never found any human being uninteresting. Even as a child, no human being was ever uninteresting to me. And I know that I could never have educated that boy if I had not found all human beings interesting.

It is this breadth of interest that permeates the teachers' conferences in a Waldorf school. It gives them atmosphere, so that a "psychological" mood prevails throughout, and the conferences thus lead to a school based on a deep psychology. It is interesting to see how, year after year, the whole college of teachers is able to deepen its capacity for psychological perception. In addition to all that I have described so far, something else must be said when we consider individual classes. We do not put much stock in statistics; for us, the classes themselves are "living beings," not just the individual students. We can take a particular class and study it, and it is very interesting to observe the imponderables that come to light. When we study a class this way, and when the teachers of various classes discuss the characteristics of each class in their college meetings, it is interesting to discover that a class having more girls than boys, for example (ours is a coeducational school), is a completely different being from that of a class in which there are more boys than girls. A class that consists of an equal number of boys and girls is yet another completely different being. This is all extremely interesting, not only because of the talk that takes place among the children themselves or the little love affairs that always occur in the higher classes. Here we must acquire the right kind of observation to notice it when necessary, and otherwise not see it. Apart from this, however, the imponderable "being" composed of the different masculine and feminine individuals gives the class a definite spiritual structure.

This is how we become familiar with the individuality of various classes. And if there are parallel classes, as happens in the Waldorf school, when necessary (and it is seldom necessary) it is possible to alter the division of the classes. Such studies in connection with the classes form the usual substance of the teachers' conferences. Thus, the conferences consist not only of school administration, but also provide a living continuation of education within the school itself, so that the teachers are always learning. Thus the conferences are the soul of the whole school. We learn to estimate trivialities correctly, to give the appropriate weight to important matters, and so on. As a result, there will not be an outcry when some child commits a small infraction; but there will be awareness when something happens that might endanger the school's development.

So the overall picture of our Waldorf school is an interesting one, and it has taken years to come about. By and large, our children, once they reach the higher classes, are better able than those at other schools when it comes to understanding what a child must learn in school. On the other hand, as I described, in the lower classes the children remain somewhat behind in reading and writing, because our methods are different and are extended over several years. Between the ages of thirteen and fifteen, however, our children begin to outpace the students of other schools. Among other reasons, this is because of the ease with which they are able to enter things with a certain aptitude for understanding.

Here, a real difficulty arises. It is a remarkable fact that where there is a light, objects create shadows. With a weak light come weak shadows; with a strong light come strong shadows. Similarly, when it comes to certain soul qualities, we can make an observation. If teachers take enough care in establishing contact with their students in every way possible, becoming models for the children's behavior, then, conversely, because of a lack of contact it can easily happen that deviations from moral conduct may appear. We should have no illusions about this; it is true. This is why so much depends on a complete "growing together" of the teacher's and student's individualities, so that a strong inner connection is felt by the children for their teachers, which is felt reciprocally by the teachers, thus assuring the development of both.

These things need to be studied in an inner, human, and loving way. Otherwise we encounter surprises. But the nature of the method tends to draw out everything that lies latent in human beings. Sometimes this is exemplified in a strange way. There is a German poet who knew that he had been brought up and taught badly. As a result, many of his inherent qualities could not be expressed, and he always complained about this. Why was this? His body had become stiff and hardened. During his youth, there was no effort to develop his individuality. One day he went to a phrenologist. (I'm not promoting phrenology, though it has some significance when practiced intuitively.) The phrenologist felt his head and had all sorts of nice things to say; these could be found, of course. At one spot of the skull, however, he stopped suddenly; he became red and did not trust himself to say anything. The poet said, "Come on, speak up; it is my predisposition to theft. It seems that if I had been better educated in school, this tendency for stealing might have led to very serious consequences."

If we wish to educate, we must have plenty of elbow room. This, however, is not provided in conventional schools, run according to the dreaded schedules of eight o'clock to nine for religion; nine to ten for gymnastics; ten to eleven for history; and math from eleven to twelve. Later classes blot out the earlier ones, and despite this teachers must get results and are driven to despair. This is why Waldorf schools have so-called teaching blocks. The children come to class. Every day during main lesson—which continues for most of the morning, from eight o'clock until ten or eleven with short recreational breaks—students are taught one subject. This is taught by one teacher, even in the higher classes. The subject is not changed each hour, but continued as long as needed for the teachers to go through what they wish to bring to the class. In arithmetic, for example, these blocks might last four weeks. Every day, from eight to ten o'clock, the subject is taken further, and one day's lesson is linked to that of the previous day. No lesson blots out an earlier one; concentration is thus enabled. After about four weeks, when arithmetic has been taken far enough and concluded, a history period might follow for another four or five weeks, again according to the time required. And so it goes on.

Our perspective is the opposite of the "specialized" teacher. When visiting the Waldorf school, you might find Dr. Baravalle taking a class for descriptive geometry.[*] The students sit facing him with their drawing boards in front of them. He lets them draw, and his manner is that of an exemplary specialized teacher of geometry. Now, when you enter another school and look at the list of professors and teachers, you will find various credentials—diplomas in Geometry, Mathematics, and so on. I have known many teachers, specialists in mathematics for example,

---

[*] Dr. Hermann von Baravalle, a teacher from the first Waldorf school in Stuttgart, helped establish the Waldorf School of Garden City, New York. During the Nazi occupation of Germany, he moved to England and then to New York. He is the author of *Geometric Drawing and theWaldorf School Plan* (published by Rudolf Steiner College Press).

who bragged that on school outings they were unable to name various plants. But it's still morning at school, and you find Dr. Baravalle walking among the desks giving an English lesson. From the whole manner of his teaching, you hear him speak about many different things, and there is no way of knowing his specialty. Some may think geography is his subject, or geometry, or something else. The essential substance and meaning of one's teaching material can undoubtedly be learned very quickly if you have a gift for getting right into that area of knowledge and experiencing it in the soul. So we have no schedule. Of course, there is nothing pedantic about this. In our Waldorf school, the main lesson is given in blocks; other lessons, of course, must fit into a schedule, but they follow the main lesson.

We also believe it is very important to teach the children two foreign languages, beginning when they first come to school as little children. We teach them French and English. Admittedly, this can be very difficult, because so many students have entered the school since it began. For example, students arrived who should enter class six, in which there are children who are already considerably advanced in languages. The new children should join them, but because they lack any notion of foreign languages we have to place them in class five. We are always dealing with such problems.

We also try to arrange the day so that the most basic lessons are taught in the morning. Consequently, physical education classes (gymnastics, eurythmy, and so on) are delayed until afternoon. But this is not a rigid rule; we cannot afford an unlimited number of teachers, so we must schedule classes as circumstances allow. Do not misunderstand me when I say that one cannot begin with ideals; do not say that spiritual science lacks ideals. We recognize the value of ideals, but they do not belong at the beginning. We can describe them beautifully, and we can say how things ought to be. We can even flatter ourselves that we are working in this direction. But in fact, we have to deal with a specific, concrete school that has eight hundred children we know and forty or fifty teachers we must also know. You might ask, however, why we have a college of teachers if none of its members correspond to the ideal. Basically, we deal with what we have, and we progress according to the facts. If we want to do something practical, we have to consider reality. This is what I had to say about the teaching blocks.

Because of our free approach to teaching—and this must be obvious from what I have been saying—it naturally happens that children do not always sit still like mice. You should see how the moral atmosphere and essence of a class depends on the one in charge. Again, it is the imponderable that counts. In this sense, I must say that there are teachers in the Waldorf school who prove inadequate in certain ways. I will not describe those, but it can happen that one enters a class and becomes aware that it is out of tune. A quarter of the class is lying under their seats, another quarter is on top of them and the rest will be running out of the room and knocking on the door from outside. This shouldn't be a mystery to us; it can be be straightened out if we know how to go along with the children. We should allow them to satisfy their urge to move; we shouldn't rely on punishment, but correct the situation in another way.

Not all of us are in favor of giving orders; on the contrary, some of us think that things should be allowed to develop naturally. And because of this, something begins to develop naturally, which I described as living within the teachers themselves. Children can certainly make a lot of noise, but this simply demonstrates their vitality. They can also be very active and lively while doing what is appropriate, so long as teachers know how to pique their interest. We should employ the good qualities of the "good" children in ways that help them learn; and with the mischievous children, we should use their unruly qualities in ways that help them progress. We will not get anywhere if we are able to develop only the children's "good" qualities. Occasionally, we must develop their mischievous qualities, while directing them in the appropriate ways. Often it is the so-called mischievous qualities that indicate strength later on; these are the very qualities that, if handled correctly, can become the most excellent qualities in the adult. Thus, we must always determine whether a child gives little trouble because of "goodness" or because of some illness. If we are concerned only with our own convenience, it is easy to think of sick children as "good," just because they sit quietly and require little attention. But when we look into human nature with real insight, we often find that we must devote much more attention to those children than we do to the "bad" children. Here, too, it is a matter of psychological insight and treatment from a spiritual perspective.

There is something else to consider. In Waldorf schools, almost all teaching takes place in the school itself; the burden of homework is lifted, since the children are given little to do at home. Thus, because the work is done with the teachers, the children's attitude is remarkable. In Waldorf schools, something like this typically happens: There were some students once who misbehaved. A teacher who was not yet fully imbued with the Waldorf method of education thought that the children should be punished, and he did this in an intellectual way. He told them, "You must stay in after school and do some arithmetic." But the children could not understand why arithmetic would be considered a punishment, since it gave them such pleasure. So the whole class (and this did happen) asked him if they could stay as well. This was intended as a punishment.

You can see how one's whole mental attitude must change completely; children should never feel that they are being punished by doing something they happily do with devotion and joy. Our teachers discover all sorts of ways of eliminating inappropriate behavior. Dr. Stein—who is especially creative in this way—once noticed that, during a lesson in his upper class, the children were writing and passing notes to one another.[*] What was his response? He began to tell them about the postal service. He explained it in detail and in such a way that the notes gradually ceased. His description of the postal service and the origin of correspondence seemed to have nothing to do with the behavior he noticed, but it was related nonetheless. You see, if instead of rationalizing our response we take advantage of a sudden inspiration that arises from our instinctive knowledge of how to deal with a class, the consequences are often beneficial. In this way, we can accomplish a lot more toward correcting the students than we could by resorting to punishment.

Above all, it must be obvious to every student in every class that their teachers live in true harmony with their own rules. For example, if a choleric boy happens to mess

---

[*] Dr. Walter Johannes Stein (1891–1957), the history teacher at the Stuttgart Waldorf school from 1919 to 1932. He was also the author of *The Ninth Century and the Holy Grail* (London: Temple Lodge, 2001).

up his exercise book, grab his neighbor by the ears, or pull someone's hair, his teacher should never shout at him for losing his temper or behaving badly. And the teacher must never threaten to hurt him. This is an extreme example, but something like this might happen when teachers fail to realize that they themselves must set the example for what they expect of the students. What we *are* is far more important than our principles and what we know. The kind of person we are is the most important thing. When candidates are expected to show that they **are** suited to the profession of teaching, if we test them in a way that examines only what they know, later on they will have to research their textbooks again to recall that knowledge. But there is no need to take an examination. In reality, no one should enter a school who does not have the personality of a teacher—in body, soul, and spirit. Because of this, I can say that when I have to choose teachers for the college of teachers at the Waldorf school, I certainly do not consider it an obstacle if someone has a teacher's diploma. In a sense, however, I look more for those whose attitude indicates a true teacher than I do for those who have passed an examination. Those who have passed examinations always concern me; of course they are smart, but this must be so despite having passed various tests.

It is remarkable the way karma works. Waldorf schools are supposed to exemplify the kind of education based on knowledge of the human being, and in fact this was possible only in Wurttemberg and nowhere else. This is because, when we were preparing to open the school there, a very old school regulation was still in effect. At the time, we would have been unable to create a Waldorf school if people had been bound by the "enlightened"

ideas that arose later from the legislature of the Weimar National Assembly, with which we have had to deal ever since as a result of its attempts to destroy our lower classes.

It will become increasingly rare that teachers are assessed as human individuals instead of according to qualifications. It will become even rarer that the lower classes will be free to act in certain ways. The world is working, as it were, toward "freedom" and "human dignity." Such "human dignity," however, is advanced in a strange way by the schedule and general arrangement of classes. In a country's capital city, there is a department of education, and this department knows what is taught in each school and class because it regulates the way subjects are delegated. As a consequence, even in the most remote school, if the teachers need to know what will be taught in the fifth grade on the twenty-first of July at 9:30 A.M., they can simply look it up in the record of the education department, and it will tell them exactly what will be taught.

In our case, however, we have two parallel classes: 5-A and 5-B. You could go into both classes, one after the other, and you would astonished by the fact that in each class something completely different is taking place. They are not even similar. Each class is entrusted entirely to the the class teacher's individuality; both teachers are allowed to do whatever corresponds to their own individuality, and this is what they do. Despite the fact that there is absolute agreement on essential matters during the teachers' conferences, there is no requirement that one class should be taught in the same way as a parallel class. What we are trying to accomplish must be done in a myriad of ways; it is never a matter of external regulations.

Thus, you will find that a teacher of the little children in class one may move in a certain way to help them find a way into drawing with a paintbrush and painting. You can enter a class and see children making all sorts of movements with their hands, and this leads to mastering the brush or pencil. Or you see the children dancing around so that some skill may be drawn from the movement of their legs. Teachers do what they think is best for the individual children and for themselves as individuals. Thus, life is brought into the class, forming a foundation that helps the children feel that they truly belong with their teachers.

Despite the old school regulation, even in Wurttemberg there are school inspections; but we have done well in this regard. The attitude of the inspectors showed real understanding, and they agreed to everything once they saw our methods and the reasons for them. But such occasions also led to some unique events. For example, the inspectors visited a class in which the teacher usually had trouble maintaining discipline. Again and again, she would have to interrupt her teaching and work hard to reestablish order. But when the government inspectors came to her class, the teacher was astonished by the children's perfect behavior. They had become model students—to the degree that, the next day, she had to say, "Children, you were so good yesterday!" And the whole class exclaimed, "Of course, Doctor; we will never let *you* down!" Something mysterious develops in students when teachers try to practice what I have mentioned at the end of these lectures. If one teaches in a way that is alive and communicates life, then life emerges, develops, and prospers.

6 | Parent-Teacher Meetings

July 22, 1924

$\mathcal{B}$efore going any further with our discussion of methods, I would like to add something to what I said yesterday about teachers' conferences. We attach great importance to our relationship with the parents of children at our Waldorf school. And to ensure complete harmony, we schedule frequent parents' evenings, attended by the parents of children living in the neighborhood. At these meetings, we discuss the intentions, methods, and arrangements of the school—in a somewhat general way, of course. And, to the degree that such gatherings allow, the parents are able to express their wishes and receive a sympathetic hearing. Thus, we have an opportunity to determine our educational goals and, moreover, do this within the social context from which those goals originated. The teachers listen to the parents' ideas about their children's education, and the parents hear (we always speak to them in a sincere and candid way) about events in the school, our thoughts on the children's education and future, and why we need schools that advance a free approach to education. In other words, this leads to a mutual understanding between the teachers and parents that arises

because we maintain human contact that is not just abstract and intellectual. We feel this kind of connection is very important, because this is all that we can rely upon. In a state school, everything is strictly regulated; we know exactly the goals that teachers must bear in mind; we know, for example, that a child of nine must reach a certain standard and so on. Everything is planned with precision.

In our case, everything depends on the free individuality of each teacher. Insofar as I am considered the school's director, nothing is given in the form of rules and regulations. In fact, there is no school director in the usual sense; each teacher is sovereign. Instead of a school director or administrator, we have teachers' conferences, where the teachers study and work in common toward progress. Consequently, there is a concrete spirit that lives and works freely in the college of teachers. It is not tyrannical, nor does it issue statements, rules, or programs; rather, it exerts its will to continually advance and improve the teachers' ability to meet the needs of teaching.

Today, our teachers have no idea what will be good for the Waldorf school five years later, because, during those years, they will learn much, and from that knowledge they will have to reassess what is or is not correct. This is why Waldorf schools are indifferent toward associations for school reform and what they consider important. Educational matters cannot be determined intellectually; they should arise only from the experience of teaching. The college of teachers works through experience. But just because this is the situation—because we live in a state of flux in terms of what we want—we need a different kind of support system than that of ordinary schools, which is given by educational authorities who dictate what schools do. We require the support of the social context in which the children are growing up. We need the inner support of the parents, because questions always come up when children come to school, and they come from the homes of their parents.

If the goal is to create individual and harmonious relationships, teachers may be even more concerned with the welfare of the children than the parents themselves, from whom they seek support. When receiving a child of seven into school, our teachers take on much more than expected if they go beyond merely taking in the parents' information—which provides little—but show further interest by visiting the parents at home. Teachers have the fathers, the mothers, and others in the children's lives; they are like shadows in a child's background. Teachers are almost as involved with those people as they are with the children themselves—especially when it comes to physical pathologies. Teachers must take this all into account and work it out for themselves; they must look at the whole situation to truly understand the children, and above all, they must be clear about what they need to do in relation to a child's environment. By visiting the parents at home, the teachers build a bridge between themselves and the parents, and this becomes a support that is social and, at the same time, free and alive.

Home visits are necessary if we want to nurture a feeling in the parents that nothing should undermine the natural sense for authority that children should feel toward their teachers. The college of teachers and the parents must work hard together to reach an understanding that is imbued with feeling soul qualities. Moreover, parents must get to know the teachers thoroughly and break any tendency to be jealous of them, because most parents are in fact jealous of their children's teachers. They feel as if the teachers want to take the children away from them; but as soon as this feeling arises, nothing can be accomplished with the children educationally. These things can be corrected, however, if teachers understand how to gain real support from the parents. This is what I wanted to add to my previous remarks on the purpose of teachers' conferences.

Now we must consider something else; we must begin to understand the times in the lives of children that are important points of transition. I spoke of one such point already—when imaginative and pictorial teaching must move on and teach children about the nature of the plants. This point comes around the age of nine or ten. It manifests in children as an inner restlessness, and they begin to ask all sorts of questions. The questions are not usually all that important in terms of their subject matter, but it is very important to note that the children have begun to feel a need to ask questions.

The relationship we establish with children at this time has great importance for their whole life. What is living in the souls of these children? We can observe it in every child who is not suffering a pathology. Before this age, any child who has not been harmed by outer influences will naturally accept the authority of the teacher; healthy children who have not been convinced of all kinds of nonsense will have a healthy respect for every adult. They look up to adults and accept them naturally as authorities. Recall your own childhood and think about what it means, especially for young children, to feel good about doing what an adult does because that person is good and worthy. Children need nothing more than to place themselves under an authority.

In a sense, this feeling is shaken somewhat between nine and ten through the development of human nature itself. It is important to have the capacity to perceive this clearly. It is a time when human nature experiences something special; it does not become conscious in children, but lives in vague sensations and feelings. Children cannot express this, but it is present nonetheless. And what do these children think unconsciously? Earlier, they might have said instinctively: If my teacher says something is good, it must be good; if my teacher says something is bad, it is bad; if my teacher says something is correct, then it must be correct; if my teacher says it is wrong, it has to be wrong. If my teacher is pleased by something, then it is beautiful; if my teacher says something is ugly and unpleasant, then it is ugly.

It is quite natural for young children to see their teachers as models, but between nine and ten their inner certainty is shaken somewhat. In their feeling life, children begin to inquire about the source of the teacher's authority. Who is the authority over the teacher, and what is the source of that authority? At this point, children begin to sense an inner urge to penetrate the visible human being—who has been a god to them—and discover what stands behind the person as a suprasensory, invisible god or divine being. Now teachers must face the children and, in a simple way, try to confirm this feeling in them. They must approach the children so that they sense something suprasensory that supports their teacher. Teachers must not speak in an arbitrary way, because they are messengers of the divine.

You must make children aware of this, but certainly not by preaching. You can only hint through words; nothing is accomplished by a pedantic approach. But you can achieve something by approaching the children and saying something of no particular importance. You might say a few words that are unimportant, but spoken in a tone of voice that suggests you have a heart, and this heart believes in what stands behind it. You must make the children aware that you are standing within the universe, but this must be done in the right way. Even if they are still unable to absorb abstract, rational ideas, they do have enough understanding to come and ask you how they, too, can know.

Children of this age often come with such questions. Now you might say: Just think; all that I am able to give you, I receive from the Sun. If the Sun did not exist, I would be unable to give you anything at all. And while we sleep, if the divine power of the Moon were not there to preserve all that we receive from the Sun, I would be unable to give you anything. In terms of meaning, you have not said anything particularly important. But if you say it with such warmth that the children feel your love for the Sun and Moon, then you can lead them beyond the stage of asking such questions, and in general this holds for all of life.

You must realize that these critical points occur in children's lives. A new feeling arises naturally. Until now, you told stories about a fir and an oak, about a buttercup and a dandelion, or about a sunflower and a violet. You spoke about nature in fairytales and thus you led the children into a world of spirit. Now it is time to tell stories from the Gospels. If you begin this earlier or try to teach them anything religious, it destroys something in children; but if you begin this when they are trying to break through to the spirit world, you can accomplish something that children demand with their whole being.

Where can you find a book that tells teachers what teaching really is? It is the children themselves who form that book. We should not learn teaching methods from any book except the one that opens before us as the children themselves. In order to read in this book, however, we need the broadest possible interest in each individual child, and nothing must divert us from this. This is where teachers are likely to experience difficulties, and these must be overcome consciously.

Imagine a teacher who has children of her own. She is faced with a more direct and difficult task than if she had no children. She must be even more aware and, above all, not believe—not even subconsciously—that all children should be like hers. She must ask herself whether all people who have children subconsciously believe that every child should be like theirs.

We can see that teachers must acknowledge something that touches the most intimate threads of one's soul life. And unless you can go into these intimate, subconscious threads, you will never gain real access to children and win their full confidence. Children suffer untold damage by believing that other children are the teacher's favorites. This must be avoided at all costs. It is not as easy to avoid as one might think, but it can be avoided by teachers who are imbued with the principles that arise from a spiritual scientific knowledge of the human being. Then, such questions discover their own solutions.

There is something that requires special attention in relation to the theme I chose for this lecture course. It is connected with the importance of education for the whole world and for humankind itself. It is the very nature of human existence that teachers—who are so involved with children and generally have so little time to live outside of those activities—require support from the outer world and must look out into the larger world. Why do teachers dry up so easily? It is because they must always bend to the level of the children. We certainly have no reason to make fun of teachers who, because they are limited to the usual concept of teaching, become dried up. Nevertheless, we should see where the danger lies, and anthroposophic teachers are in a position to be especially aware of this. If the ordinary teachers' notion of history gradually becomes like a textbook (which can happen in just a few years), where should they look for other ideas that are truly human? What is the remedy? What little time teachers are left with after a school week is usually spent recovering from fatigue, and frequently it is merely popular politics that form their attitudes about matters of world importance. Consequently, the soul life of such teachers is not turned outward with the kind of understanding needed by people between, say, thirty and forty. Furthermore, they do not keep fit and well by thinking that the best way to recuperate during leisure hours is to play cards or do something else that has no connection with a spiritual life.

The situation for teachers whose life is permeated with spiritual science is very different. Their perspective on the world continually broadens; their vision continues to extend further. It is easy to show how such things affect each other. It manifests in the most enthusiastic anthroposophists—for example, one who becomes a history teacher and tends to carry spiritual scientific views into history lessons, thus making the mistake of teaching anthroposophy instead of history. This must also be avoided. This problem can be completely avoided by teachers who, with the children on the one hand and anthroposophy on the other, feel the need to build a bridge between the school and the homes of parents. Although spiritual science is knowledge and understanding applied to the human being, there are nevertheless necessities in life that must be observed.

What is the common thinking today, influenced as people are by current ideas about educational reform or by revolutionary ideas in this area? I will not go into what socialists have to say, but will limit myself to the thinking of the upper middle classes. They seem to think that people should get out of the city and move to the country, so that children can be properly educated away from town. It is felt that this is the only way children can develop in a natural way. And so it goes. But how does such thinking fit with more comprehensive view of the world? It is really an admission of personal helplessness.

The important point is not to invent some way to educate a number of children apart from the world and according to one's own intellectual, abstract ideas. Rather, the point is to discover how we can help children grow into real human beings in society, which is indeed their environment. We must gather our strength and not remove children from the society in which they live. It is essential to have such courage. This is connected with the significance of education in the world.

There must also be a deep sense that the world should find its way into the school. The world must always exist within the school, though in a childlike way. So, if we stand for healthy education, we should not invent all kinds of activities intended only for children. All sorts of things are devised for children to do. For example, they must learn to braid; they must perform all kinds of meaningless activities that are completely unrelated to life—

just to keep the children busy. Such methods never serve any real purpose in the children's development. Rather, all play at school should imitate life; everything must come from life, with nothing invented. So, despite the good intentions behind them, things such as those introduced by Fröbel or others to educate little children are really unrelated to child development.* These are inventions that belong to our age of rationalism, and theories should not form the basis of a school's activities. Above all, there must be a hidden sense that life rules everything in education. In this sense, our experiences can be quite remarkable.

I told you that when children reach the age of changing teeth their education should be smoothed through painting or drawing. Writing, a form of drawing that has become abstract, should be developed through painted drawings or drawn paintings. It should be kept in mind, however, that children are very sensitive to aesthetic impressions. There are little artists hiding in them, and some very interesting discoveries can be made. A truly good teacher may be placed in charge of a class—one who is ready to do what I have described, one who is filled with enthusiasm and ready to do away with earlier methods of education and to educate in this new way. Such teachers begin with this method of painted drawings or drawn paintings. The jars of paint and the paintbrushes are prepared, and the children pick up their brushes. Now you may experience something like this: You have no idea of the difference between a color that shines and one that does not; you are too old. In this way, you can have an odd experience.

---

* Friedrich Wilhelm August Fröbel (1782–1852), educator and advocate for kindergarten, devised play methods for the early education.

I once had the opportunity of telling an excellent chemist about our efforts to produce radiant, shining colors for the paintings in the Goetheanum and how we were experimenting with colors made from plants.[*] He replied, "But we can already do much better than that; today we have the means to produce colors that are iridescent and begin to shimmer when it is dark." That chemist did not understand anything I was saying; he immediately thought in terms of chemistry. Adults often lack any sense of "shining" color. Children still have this sense. If you can read in the nature of childhood what they still possess, everything goes along wonderfully with very few words. The guidance of teachers must arise through an approach that is understanding and artistic. In this way, children easily find their way into everything their teachers wish to bring them. None of this can be brought about unless we can feel deeply that our school is a place for young life. At the same time, we must recognize what is appropriate for adult life. We must cultivate a sensitivity as to what can and cannot be done.

Now, please do not be offended by what I am about to say. Last year, in the context of a conference on anthroposophic education, the following incident occurred. There was the desire to show a public audience eurythmy, which plays such an important role in our education. This was done, but by children who gave a demonstration of what they had learned at school in eurythmy lessons. A performance showing eurythmy as an art was given later on. The arrangements did not allow people the opportunity to gain some understanding of eurythmy as introduced to the school. It was done the other way around;

---

[*] The Goetheanum, designed by Rudolf Steiner, is the headquarters for the Anthroposophical Society in Dornach, Switzerland.

the children's eurythmy demonstration was given first. As a result, the audience was unconvinced and had no idea what it was all about. Just imagine that, until now, there had been no art of painting; then, suddenly, an exhibition is held that shows children's first attempts with colors. Those outside the anthroposophic movement could not see in that children's demonstration the true intentions behind anthroposophy and eurythmy. Such a demonstration has no meaning unless eurythmy is introduced first as an art; then people can see its role in life and its significance in the world of art. And the importance of eurythmy in education can also be recognized. Otherwise, people may see eurythmy as just another of the many whimsical ideas in the world.

These things must lead us not only to prepare ourselves to work in education in the old, narrow sense, but to work with a somewhat broader view, so that school is not separated from life but an integral part of it. This is just as important as inventing some clever method in education. I have repeatedly stressed the fact that it is the mental attitude that counts—a mental attitude and a gift of insight.

Obviously, not everything is equally perfect; this goes without saying. I ask you not to misunderstand what was just said, and this applies to anthroposophists as well. I appreciate everything that is done—as it is here—with such willing sacrifice. However, if I had not spoken in this way, something like the following could occur. Wherever there is strong light, there are strong shadows; so wherever efforts are made toward the more spiritual accomplishments, there the darkest shadows also arise. The danger is not less than in conventional groups, but greater. And, if we wish to be up to the tasks that confront us in a life that is becoming increasingly complex, we must be especially awake and aware of what life requires of humankind. We no longer have those sharply defined traditions that guided earlier humanity. We can no longer be content with what our ancestors considered right; we must raise our children so that they can form their own judgments. Thus it is imperative that we break through the narrow confines of our preconceived ideas and take a stand in the larger life and work of the world.

We must no longer look for simple concepts with which to explain the most important questions of life. For the most part, even when there is no wish to be pedantic, people try to explain most things by using superficial definitions, in pretty much the same way they did in a certain school of Greek philosophy. People asked: What is a human being? The answer was that a human being is a living being who stands on two legs and has no feathers. Even today, many definitions are based on the same reasoning. Someone, however, did some hard thinking about what might be behind such portentous words. The next day, he brought a plucked goose. Here was a being able to stand on two legs and lacking feathers, and the student now asserted that this was a human being.

This is an extreme example of what you find in Goethe's play, *Goetz von Berlechingen,* in which a little boy begins to describe what he knows about geography. When he comes to his own area, he describes it according to his lesson book, and then goes on to describe a man whose development took place in this same neighbourhood. But he lacks the foggiest idea that this man is his father. Out of sheer erudition, based on a book, he does not recognize his own father. Nevertheless, an experience I once had in Weimar goes even further. In Weimar, there are, of course, newspapers. They are produced in the usual way of small places. Bits and pieces of suitable news are cut from newspapers of larger towns and inserted into the small town paper. Once, on January 22, we read this item of news in Weimar: "Yesterday, there was a violent thunderstorm over our city." But this bit of news had been taken from the *Leipzig Nachrichten*.

Such things happen, and we are continually caught in their web of confusion. People theorize in abstract concepts. They study the theory of relativity and get the idea that it makes no difference whether a man drives a car to Osterbeek or Osterbeek comes to him. But if we wish to reach a conclusion based on reality, we would have to say that, if the car is not used it does not suffer wear and tear, and the driver does not get tired. But if the opposite happens, the effect will probably be the opposite. If we think in this way, without comparing every line and movement, commonsense tells us that our own being changes when it goes from a state of rest to a condition of movement. Keeping in mind the kind of thinking that prevails today, it's no wonder that a theory of relativity develops when attention is turned to things in isolation. If we return to reality, however, it becomes obvious that there is no connection between reality and theories based on mere relationships. Whether or not we are educated or smart today, we continue to live outside reality; we live in a world of ideas, much as the little boy in *Goetz von Berlechingen*, who did not recognize his father, despite the description of him in the geography book. Our way of life lacks direct contact with reality.

This is exactly what we must bring to school; we must face this direct impact of reality. We can best do this if we understand everything related to the real nature of the human being. For this reason, I have repeatedly pointed out how easy it is for people to assert today that children should be taught pictorially, through object lessons, and that nothing should be presented to them that is beyond their immediate comprehension. In doing so, however, we are drawn into the most objectionable trivialities—I have already mentioned the calculator.

Now consider this example: At the age of eight, I take something in, but I do not really understand it. All I know is that my teacher says so, and I love my teacher. He is my natural authority. Because he has said it, I accept it wholeheartedly. At the age of fifteen, I still do not understand it. But when I reach thirty-five, I encounter an experience that recalls, as though from wonderful spiritual depths, what I did not understand when I was eight, but that I accepted solely on the authority of the teacher I loved. Because he was my authority, I felt certain that it must be true. Now life brings me another experience and suddenly, in a flash, I understand the earlier one. All this time, it was hidden within me, and now life grants me the possibility of understanding it. Such experiences lead to a tremendous sense of obligation. One has to say that it is indeed sad for those who have no experience of such moments in life, when something arises from one's inner being into consciousness, something accepted long ago on the basis of authority but not understood until later. No one should be deprived of such experiences, because in later years, it is a source of enthusiastic and purposeful activity in life.

But let us add something else. I said that, between the change of teeth and puberty, children should not be given moral precepts; instead, we should be careful to ensure that the good pleases them because it pleases their teacher, and the bad displeases them because it displeases their teacher. During the second period of life, everything should be based on an affinity for goodness and an aversion toward evil. Moral feelings are implanted deeply in the soul, establishing a sense of moral well-being when experiencing benevolence and a sense of moral discomfort in experiencing malevolence.

Then comes the time of puberty. Just as walking is fully developed during the first seven years, and speech during the next seven years, so during the third seven-year period, thinking comes into its own and becomes independent. This takes place only with the beginning of puberty; then we become truly capable of forming a judgment. At this time, if feelings have been planted in us and a good foundation has been laid as I indicated, then we begin to form thoughts out of an inner urge, and we are able to form judgments. For example, when something pleases me, I am bound to act in accordance with it; if it displeases me, it is my duty to leave it alone. The significance of this is that *duty itself grows out of pleasure and displeasure;* it is not instilled in me, but arises from pleasure and displeasure.

This is the awakening of true freedom in the human soul. We experience freedom because our sense of morality is the deepest single impulse of the human soul. When children have been led through natural authority to a sense of morality so that morality lives in the world of feeling, then after puberty the idea of duty functions from the inner human individual. This is a healthy process. This is how we lead children correctly to the point where they can experience individual freedom. People lack this experience today, because they are unable to have it— because, before puberty, knowledge of good and evil was instilled into them; they were indoctrinated with what they should or should not do. Moral instruction pays no attention to the right approach, and it gradually dries up human beings, makes them into "skeletons" of moral precepts, on which one's conduct in life is hung like clothes on a hanger.

Life cannot form a harmonious whole unless education follows a course that is different from the usual one. It must be understood that children go through one stage between birth and the change of teeth, another between the change of teeth and puberty, and yet another between puberty and the age of twenty-one. Why do children do one thing or another during the period before the age of seven? Because they have a desire to imitate; they want to do everything they see done in their immediate surroundings. But what they do must be connected with life; it must lead to the activity of life. We can do much to bring this about if we accustom children to feeling gratitude for what they receive from their environment. Gratitude is the essential virtue in children between birth and the change of teeth. They should see that everyone who has some relationship to them in the world shows gratitude for what they receive from this world. If, in confronting the outer world and wanting to imitate it, children see gestures of gratitude, it helps to establish the right moral human attitude in them. Gratitude belongs to the first seven years of life.

If gratitude has been developed in children during the first period, then between seven and fourteen, it is easy to develop what must become the motivating impulse—*love*—in everything they do. Love is the virtue that belongs to the second period of life. And after puberty, the experiences of love between the change of teeth and puberty become *duty,* the most inner of human motivations. It becomes the guiding line for life. Goethe once expressed this beautifully when he asked, "What is duty? It is when we love what we demand of ourselves." This is the goal we must attain. But we cannot reach it unless we are guided to it by the stages of gratitude, love, and duty.

A few days ago, we saw how things arise from an earlier period of life and carry into later ones. I spoke of this when I answered a question. Now I must explain that this also has a good side; it is something that must happen. Of course, I do not mean that gratitude should cease at seven, or love at fourteen. But this is the very secret of life—what we developed in one period can be carried over into later ones, but it will metamorphos, intensify, and change. We would be unable to carry over the good of one period if it were impossible to bring along the bad as well. But education must be concerned with this. It should ensure that the inherent human forces that enable us to carry over something from an earlier to a later period are used to advance goodness. To accomplish this, however, we must use what I spoke of yesterday.

Consider the case of a child in whom there is a possibility of moral weakness in later life because of certain pathological tendencies. We perceive that goodness does not really please him, nor does malevolence awaken displeasure in him. In this respect, he does not progress. Then, because love cannot develop in the right way between seven and fourteen, we try to use what is inherent in human nature itself; we try to develop a real sense of gratitude in the child, educating him so that he turns with true gratitude to the natural authority of his teacher. When we do this, matters will also improve in the realm of love. Knowledge of human nature prevents us from doing things in such a way that we say a boy lacks love for goodness and an aversion toward evil—therefore, I must instill this in him. This cannot be done. But this happens on its own if we foster gratitude in a child. So it is essential to understand the role of gratitude in relation to love in moral development; we must realize that gratitude develops naturally in human nature during the first years of life, and that love is active in the human organization as a soul quality before being expressed physically at puberty. What then manifests externally is already active between seven and fourteen as the deepest principle of life and growth in human beings. It lives and weaves in our inmost being.

Here, it is possible to discuss such things on a fundamental level, so I may be allowed to say what is undoubtedly a fact. Once teachers have understood the nature of an education based on real knowledge of the human being—when we are engaged in the practice of such education, on the one hand, and, on the other, whenever we are concerned with studying the anthroposophic worldview, each affects the other. Teachers must work in the school in such a way that they take it for grated that love is working inwardly in children, and comes to outer expression in sexuality.

Anthroposophic teachers also attend meetings where they study the worldview of anthroposophy. There they hear from people who have gained the necessary knowledge that comes from initiation wisdom—such as the fact that human beings consist of physical, ether, and astral bodies and an I being. Between the ages of seven and fourteen, the ether body works mainly on the physical body. The astral body descends into the physical and ether bodies at the time of puberty. There are those who are able to penetrate more deeply into these matters; they are able to perceive more than just physical processes, and their perceptions always include spiritual processes. And when these two processes are separated, they can perceive each separately. Such individuals can discern in boys of eleven or twelve how the astral body is already "sounding"—chiming, so to speak—with the deeper tone that will be heard outwardly at puberty. And a similar process takes place in the astral body of girls at eleven or twelve.

These are facts, and if they are viewed as realities, they tend to illuminate life's problems. And we can have some very remarkable experiences in relation to these things. For example, in 1906 I presented a number of lectures in Paris to a fairly small group of people.* I had prepared my lectures with these particular people in mind, considering the fact that this group included highly educated people, writers, artists, and others who, at this particular time, were concerned with specific matters. Things have changed since then, but at that time something very specific was behind the matters that commanded their attention. They were the kind of people who get up in the morning filled with the idea that they belong to a society that is interested in its literary and art history. And when you belong to such a society, you wear this sort of tie, and ever since some certain year, no one goes to parties in tails or a dinner jacket. One is aware of this when invited to dine where such topics are discussed. Then in the evening, one goes to the theater and to see plays that deal with current issues. Then, the "poets" write such plays themselves.

---

* "Esoteric Christianity: An Outline of Psychological Cosmogony," May 25–June 14 (GA 94).

Initially there is a man of deep and inward sensibility, out of whose heart these great problems arise in an upright and honourable way. There is a [Swedish poet] Strindberg. Later on, there are those who popularize Strindberg to a wider public. And so, when I held these Paris lectures, the particular problem was much discussed that had recently driven the tragic Otto Weininger (1880–1903) to commit suicide. The problem that Weininger portrays in such a childlike but noble way in *Geschlecht und Charakter* ("Sex and Character") was the problem of the day.

After I had dealt with the matters essential to an understanding of the subject, I went on to explain that every human being manifests one gender in the outer physical body, but carries the other gender in the ether body. So, a woman has a male ether body, and a man has a female ether body. Human beings, in their totality, are all double gendered; we carry the other gender within us. When something like this is said, I can actually see how people begin to look out from their astral bodies; they suddenly feel that a problem is solved, which they have chewed on for a long time. A certain restlessness, but a pleasant kind of restlessness, becomes perceptible among the audience. Where there are big problems—not just the insignificant sensations of life—where there is real enthusiasm, even if it is sometimes close to small talk, again one becomes aware of how a sense of relief, of being freed from a burden, emanates from those present.

So, teachers who are anthroposophists always view big problems as something that can work on them in such a way that they remains human at every stage of life. They do not dry up, but stay fresh and alert and able to bring that freshness with them to school. It is a completely different matter whether a teacher merely studies text-books and presents their content to the children, or whether a teacher steps out of all of that and, as a simple human being, faces the great perspectives of the world. In such cases, when such teachers enter a classroom and teach, they bring what they have absorbed into the atmosphere there.

7 | The Temperaments and the Human Organism

July 23, 1924

$\mathcal{T}$he lectures given here have described an art of education based on knowledge of the human being, and at this point you may have a clear idea of the ideal relationship between the teachers and students. The soul life and personality of teachers affect the students in hundreds of unseen ways, but this is ineffective unless a penetrating knowledge of the human being lives within the teachers' souls—a kind of knowledge that borders on spiritual experience. And because there are so many mistaken ideas about what "spiritual experience" actually is, I need to precede my lecture with a few comments to clarify what this means in an anthroposophic sense.

First, it is easy to imagine that spiritual perception must rise above all that is material. Certainly we can have a deeply satisfying soul experience by rising above the material and ascending into the spiritual world, although this may be colored by a feeling of egoism. We must do this, because we cannot become familiar with the spiritual unless we gain knowledge of the spirit world, and spiritual science must deal in many ways with spirit realms and beings that are unrelated to the physical, sensory world. And when it comes to understanding what modern humankind so urgently needs to know—about the actual suprasensory human life before birth or conception and the life after death—then we must rise to body-free, suprasensory, supraphysical perception. But, of course, we must also act and work and stand firmly in this physical world. For example, teachers are not asked to teach disembodied souls. If we want to be teachers, we do not inquire about our relationship to souls who have died and now live in the spirit world. Rather, to work as teachers between birth and death, we must inquire about how a soul lives in the physical body. We must indeed consider this, at least for the years immediately after birth. It is really a matter of being able to look with spirit into the physical. Indeed, spiritual science is primarily a matter of investigating the material world through spirit.

But the opposite process is also correct; we must use spiritual vision to penetrate the spirit world, to the degree that the spiritual seems to be as full of the "sap of life" as anything in the sensory world. We must be able to speak of the spirit world as if it radiated colors, as if its sounds could be heard, as if it were just as embodied as beings in the sensory world. In anthroposophy, it is mainly this that annoys abstract philosophers so much. They find it very irritating that spiritual investigators describe the world of spirit beings as if one might meet such beings at any moment, just as we might meet a person, as if one might hold out a hand to them or speak with them. Spiritual researchers describe spirit beings as though they were physical beings, and indeed their description makes such beings seem almost earthly. In other words, they portray the spirit in pictures that the senses can comprehend.

They do so with full consciousness, because to them spirit is absolutely real.

And there is some truth in all this, because real knowledge of the whole leads us to the point where it is possible to "give one's hand" to spirit beings; one can meet and speak with them. This strikes philosophers as paradoxical, because they can conceive of the spirit world only through abstract ideas. Nevertheless, such descriptions are needed. On the other hand, it is also necessary to "see through" human beings, so that the material aspect vanishes completely and only pure spirit remains. But if one who is not an anthroposophist wants to view human beings as spirit, they become not just a ghost, but much less. Human beings become "hangers" on which all sorts of concepts are hung in order to generate mental images and such. By comparison, a ghost is fairly solid, but a human being described by philosophers is really indecently naked when it comes to spirit.

Spiritual science sees physical human beings with purely spiritual perception, but they nevertheless retain their brains, liver, lungs, and so on. They are concrete human beings, having everything that one might find when a body is dissected. Everything that is spiritual in nature works right into the physical. The physical is observed spiritually, but human beings nevertheless have a physical body. Spiritual reality goes so far that one can even blow one's nose in a spiritual sense. The only way to bring the physical and spiritual together is by contemplating the physical in such a way that it can become completely spiritual, and by contemplating spirit so that it becomes almost physical. The physical human being can be contemplated in a state of health or illness, but the perceptible material vanishes and becomes spirit. And spirit can be contemplated as it exists between death and rebirth; in the sense of an image, it becomes physical. Thus the two are brought together.

There are two possibilities for learning to penetrate actual human beings: the possibility of seeing spirit through the use of sensory images, and the possibility of seeing actual spiritual entities within the sensory world. If one asks how to understand spirit vision in the true sense, we can say that we must learn to see everything related to the senses in a spiritual way, and we must view spirit in a way that is similar to the way in which we use our senses. This seems odd, but it is true. And you cannot view children in the right way until you have penetrated what I just said and have released its truth.

Let me give you an example. A child in my class is growing pale, and I notice an increasing pallor manifesting in the physical life of the girl. But we gain nothing by going to a doctor and getting some prescription to restore the child's color. We could call the school doctor, who comes and prescribes something to restore her lost color. But even if the doctor has done absolutely the right thing and prescribed the correct remedy, we may observe something strange in this "cured" child. In a certain sense, of course, she is cured. We could even call someone with the knowledge of a doctor to write a testimonial for the authorities, and it would probably be said that the doctor had cured the child. Later on, however, we will notice that the "cured" child can no longer absorb things properly; she is fidgety and restless and cannot pay attention. Previously, she sat quietly in her place, pale and a bit slow, but now she begins to hit her neighbor. Previously she would dip her pen gently into the ink, but now she does it with such force that the ink splatters her exercise book. The doctor acted properly, but the result was not beneficial. Sometimes people who have been "cured" suffer later on from extraordinary effects.

Again, in such cases it is important to recognize the source of the problem. When teachers are able to penetrate the spiritual cause of an outer physical expression such as pallor, they realize, for example, that the power of memory acting in the soul is really a transformed growth force. And to develop the forces of growth and nourishment is exactly the same (on a lower level) as it is to cultivate the power of memory. It is the same force, but at a different stage of metamorphosis. Pictured systematically we can say that, during the first years of a child's life, these two forces are merged and have not yet separated. Later, memory separates from this fused condition, and it becomes an independent force. The same is true of the forces of growth and nourishment. Small children still need those forces that later become memory, so that the stomach can function and digest milk; this is why they are unable to remember things. Later, when the power of memory no longer serves the stomach—when the stomach makes fewer demands and retains only a minimum of those forces—then part of the growth forces are transformed into the soul quality of memory. The other children in the class may be more robust, and the division between their powers of memory and growth may be better balanced. Consequently, the teacher pays less attention to a child who has little to fall back on in this sense. If this is the case, it may happen that the child's power of memory is overtaxed, with too much demanded of that liberated faculty. So the child becomes pale, and the teacher must recognized that has happened because too much strain has been placed on the child's memory. And the color returns when such a child is relieved of this burden. But teachers must understand that a growing pallor is connected with what they have done by overburdening the child's memory. It is important to see right into physical symptoms and to recognize that, when a child grows too pale, it is because the memory has been overtaxed.

And I may have another child in the class who occasionally becomes very red in the face, and this, too, may be a cause for concern. When a feverish red flush appears, it is easy to see certain parallel conditions in the child's soul life. In the strangest way, when we would least expect it, such children become passionately angry and overly emotional. Naturally, one could do the same as before—something may be prescribed for a rush of blood to the head. In these cases, too, a doctor's duty is performed. But it is important to recognize that, in contrast to the other, this child's memory has been neglected. The forces of memory have gone too much into the forces of growth and nourishment. Here, we must try to require more of the child's memory. If we do this, the symptoms will disappear.

Unless we consider the physical and spiritual together, there are many matters in a school that we will not recognize as needing adjustment. We can train ourselves to see this interrelationship of body and spirit by looking at the temperaments, which lies between them as part of the human organization as a whole. Children come to school, and they have four temperaments—varied, of course, with all kinds of transitions and mixes. These temperaments are called melancholic, phlegmatic, sanguine, and choleric. In Waldorf education, we greatly value the ability to enter and understand children according to their temperaments. We actually arrange the classroom seating on this basis. For example, we try to determine which children are choleric and place them together. Thus, the teachers know that one corner contains all the children who tend to be choleric. In another, the phlegmatic children are seated; somewhere in the middle are the sanguines; and somewhere else, the melancholics are in a group. This method of grouping has great advantages. Experience shows that, after a while, the phlegmatics become so bored with sitting together that, to get rid of their boredom, they begin to interact. Cholerics, on the other hand, beat up on one another, and this, too, quickly improves. It is the same for the fidgety sanguines, and the melancholics get see what it is like when others are absorbed in melancholy. Handling children in this way allows one to see how like reacts favorably to like. This is true even from an external point of view, apart from the fact that it allows teachers to survey the whole class much more easily because the children of similar temperaments are seated together.

And now we come to the essential point. Teacher must go so deeply into the nature of the human being that they are able to deal in a truly practical way with cholerics, sanguines, and melancholics. Naturally, there will be times when it is necessary to build a bridge, as I mentioned, between the school and the home, and this must be done in a friendly, tactful way. Imagine that I have a melancholic boy in class, and I can barely do anything with him. I am unable to go into his difficulties in the right way. He broods and withdraws; he is self-occupied and pays no attention to what is going on in class. If one applies educational methods that are not based on knowledge of the human being, one might think that we should do everything possible to get his attention and draw him out. In general, however this will only make things worse; the child will brood even more. All such cures, which arise from superficial thinking, are of little help. The best help in such cases is the spontaneous love that the teacher feels for the child, because this arouses an awareness of sympathy and stirs the child's subconscious. It is certain that all forms of appeal are not just wasted effort, but actually harm the child, who becomes more melancholic than before.

In class it helps greatly to enter the melancholy, discover its tendencies, and show interest in the child's mental attitude. In a sense, the teacher becomes melancholic with the melancholic child. As teachers, we must carry all four temperaments in harmonious, balanced activity. And this balance, which directly contradicts the child's melancholy, is perceived by the child if it is continued and always present in the relationship between teacher and child. Children see the kind of person their teacher is by sensing what lies behind the teacher's words. In this way, sneaking in behind this accepted mask of melancholy, the teacher's loving sympathy is implanted in the child. This can be of great help in the class.

Now we will take this even further. We must recognize that every manifestation of human melancholy is related to some irregularity in the liver function. This may seem unlikely to a physiologist, but it is true that every kind of melancholy, especially when it becomes a pathology, is a result of some irregularity of this kind. In such cases, I turn to the child's parents and tell them to put more sugar than usual into the child's food. Sweet things and sugar help to regulate the liver function. By advising a mother to give her child more sugar, the school and home work together to lift the child's melancholy out of a pathological condition, and I create the possibility of finding the right constitutional treatment.

Or I may have a sanguine girl who goes from one impression to another; she always wants what comes next, almost before she has grasped what precedes it. She starts out strong and shows great interest in everything, but interest soon fades. Such a child is generally fair rather than dark. So I am faced with the problem of how to deal with her at school. Whenever I do anything with her, I try to be more sanguine than she is. I rapidly change the way I impress her, so that she does not have to hurry from one impression to another on her own; she has to match my pace. This changes the situation, and she eventually tires of it and gives up. Between my "sanguine" impressions on the child and her rush from one thing to another according to her temperament, a more harmonious condition is gradually established in her as a natural response.

So I can treat the sanguine children this way. I present them with quickly changing impressions, always thinking up something new, so that, say, they first see black then white, and thus they have to continually hurry from one thing to another. Then I get in touch with the parents, and will hear from them that their children have an extraordinary love of sugar. Perhaps they are given many sweets or in some other way manage to get hold of them. Or perhaps the family as a whole loves sweet dishes. When this is not the case, then mother's milk may have been too sweet. So I explain this to the parents and advise them to put the sanguine children on a diet for a while by reducing their amount of sugar. Thus, by arranging a low-sugar diet with the parents, cooperation is established between home and school. The reduction of sugar will gradually help to overcome the abnormality that, in this case, is caused by an irregularity in the liver's activity in relation to gall secretions; there is a slight, barely noticeable irregularity in the secretion of gall. Here, too, I will recognize the help from the parents.

Thus, we must recognize where the physical is both united and within spirit as a fact. We can go into greater detail and describe, say, a boy who is quick to comprehend and understand everything easily, but after a few days, when I review what he grasped so quickly, and about which I was so pleased, it has vanished. Again, in this case I can do much at school to improve the situation. I will try to explain something to the boy that requires more concentration than he us used to. He us able to understand things too quickly, and he doesn't need to exert enough inner effort, so what he learns may not make a strong enough impression on him. Thus, I give him some hard nuts to crack; I give him something more difficult to understand, requiring greater attention. I can do this at school.

Again, I contact the child's parents, and I may hear various things from them. What I am saying will not be true of every case, but I want to give some idea of a path to pursued. I will have a tactful discussion with the parents, avoiding any hint of arrogance by not talking down to them when giving instructions. Through our conversation, I discover how the family eats, and I will most likely discover that this child eats too many potatoes. This situation is a little difficult, because they might tell me that, whereas their child may eat too many potatoes, the neighbor's little daughter eats even more, and she doesn't have the same problems; thus the trouble cannot be caused by eating potatoes. Something like this is what a parent may say. Nevertheless, the problem does arise from eating potatoes, because children's bodies differ from one another—one being able to assimilate more potatoes than another. The strange thing is that the condition of one child shows that too many potatoes are consumed; it is shown by the fact that the memory is not functioning as it should. In this case, however, the remedy is not fewer potatoes, though it may lead to some improvement; but after a while, matters are no better than before. An immediate reduction of potatoes does not lead to the desired effect; rather, it is a matter of breaking a habit gradually through some activity. So we suggest that the parents give the child a little less potatoes the first week; a little less for the second week; and so on, so that the child is becoming accustomed to eating only small amounts of potatoes. In this case it is a question of breaking a habit, and here we see the healing effect that can be induced by this means.

"Idealists" are very likely to criticize anthroposophy and argue that it is materialistic—and they actually do this. For example, if an anthroposophist says that a child who comprehends easily but fails to retain the material should gradually eat fewer potatoes, people will accuse that person of being an absolute materialist. Nevertheless, there is such an intimate interaction between matter and spirit that we cannot work effectively unless we can penetrate matter with spiritual perception and master it through spiritual knowledge. It is really unnecessary to say how greatly such things are slandered in today's society. But if teachers are open to a worldview that reveals broad vistas, they come to understand these things. One's outlook merely needs to be extended. For example, when you realize how little sugar is consumed in Russia compared to the amount in England, it will help you understand children. And if you compare the Russian and English temperaments, you can easily understand the effect of sugar on one's temperament. It is useful to understand the world, because such knowledge can assist us in everyday tasks.

Now I will add this. In Baden, Germany, there is a remarkable monument that honors Drake. I wanted to know what was so special about this particular Drake, so I looked it up in an encyclopedia and read: "In Offenburg, a monument was erected in memory of Sir Francis Drake, because it was erroneously believed that he had introduced potatoes into Europe." There it is in black and white. So a memorial was erected in honor of this man because he supposedly introduced potatoes to Europe. He didn't, but he has a memorial in Offenburg anyway.

The potato was introduced into Europe fairly recently. Now I will tell you something, and you can laugh as much as you like, but it is the truth, nevertheless. One can study how the development of human intelligence is recorded from well before there were potatoes until their introduction. And, as you know, potatoes are used in alcohol distilleries. Thus potatoes suddenly played an important role in the development of Europeans. If you compare the increase in the use of potatoes with the development of intelligence, you find that, compared to people today, those living before the time of potatoes had a less detailed understanding of things; but what they were able to grasp was retained. They tended to conserve knowledge, which was deeply inner. After the introduction of the potato, people began to comprehend things more quikly, but it was not retained, because knowledge did not sink in deeply enough. The history of intellectual development runs parallel to eating potatoes. So again we can see how spiritual science explains this in a material way. People everywhere can learn much about cultural history if they would only realize how the physical takes hold of the spiritual in human subconsciousness. This is easy to see in the nature of human desires.

Let us take the example of a man who has to write a great deal. Every day he has to write newspaper articles, and he feels a need to chew on his pen when trying to meet his deadlines. If you have been through this yourself, you can talk about it; but no one has a right to criticize others unless one speaks from personal experience. While pondering and biting a pen, one feels a need for coffee, since coffee helps one's thoughts cohere. Thinking becomes more logical when one drinks coffee. Journalists must enjoy coffee, because if they do not drink it, their work requires more from them.

By contrast, consider a diplomat. Just recall the diplomats before the World War and what they had to acquire. They had to use their legs in a special approved way; in the society in which they moved, they had to learn how to glide rather than step firmly as ordinary people do. And their thoughts had to become somewhat fleeting and fluid. Diplomats who have logical minds will most likely fail in that profession and be unsuccessful in their efforts to help the nations resolve problems. When diplomats are together, one does not say they are having coffee, but that they are having tea. At such times there is a need for one cup of tea after another, so that the interchange of thoughts does not proceed in logical sequence, but arises, so far as possible, from one idea to the next. This is why diplomats love to drink tea; tea releases one thought from the next; it makes thinking fluid and fleeting and destroys logic. So we may say that writers tend to love coffee, and diplomats tend to love tea, and in both cases, the instinct is appropriate. If we know this, we shall not see it as an infringement on human freedom. Logic is obviously not a product of coffee, but a subconscious aid; the soul remains free.

When we are considering children, it is especially helpful to look into relationships such as these—as when we say that tea is the drink of diplomats, coffee the drink of writers, and so on. We are also able gradually to gain an understanding of the effects produced by the potato. It places great demands on the digestion; moreover, very small, almost homeopathic doses, come from the digestive organs and go into to the brain. This "homeopathic" dose is nonetheless very potent; it stimulates the forces of abstract intelligence.

At this point, I may be permitted to reveal something else. If we examine the substance of a potato through a microscope, we see a well-known form of carbohydrate; and if we observe the astral body of one who has eaten a large portion of potatoes, we notice that in the area of the brain, a little over an inch behind the forehead, the potato substance becomes active there, forming uniform eccentric circles. The movements of the astral body become similar to the substance of the potato, and the potato eater becomes exceptionally intelligent, bubbling with intelligence, but it is transient and does not last. So, if you concede that a human being possesses spirit and soul, is it completely foolish and fantastic to speak of spirit in images from the sensory world? Those who always want to speak of spirit in abstract terms present nothing truly spiritual. It is quite the contrary in the case of those who are able to bring spirit down to earth through pictures related to the senses. Such individuals can say that, when someone bubbles with intelligence, potato substance forms in the brain, but in a spiritual sense.

In this way we learn to recognize subtle and delicate differentiations and transitions. We discover that tea affects logic by making a cleavage between thoughts, but it does not stimulate thinking. By saying that diplomats have a predilection for tea, we do not imply that they can produce thoughts. On the other hand, potatoes do stimulate thoughts. They shoot thoughts upward like lightning, only to let them vanish. But, along with this swift upsurge of thoughts (which can also take place in children), there is a parallel process that undermines the digestive system. In children whose digestive system is upset this way, leading to complaints of constipation, we see that all kinds of useless, though clever, thoughts shoot up into their heads, thoughts that they certainly lose again, but were nevertheless there.

I mention these things in detail so you can see how the soul and the physical body must be seen as a whole unity, and how, in the course of human development, a condition must be brought about again that can hold together the most varied of cultural streams. Today, we are living in a time when body and soul are completely separated from each other. We can see this clearly when we are able to look more deeply into the history of human evolution.

Today we separate religion, art, and science. The guardians of religion do everything in their power to prevent any encroachment by science into religion. They argue that religion is a matter of faith, and science belongs elsewhere. In science, nothing is based on faith; everything is based on knowledge. In order to succeed in separating them this way, spirit is cut off from science, and the world is cut off from religion; the result is that religion becomes abstract, and science eliminates spirit. And art is completely emancipated. Today, there are those who, if you say something about the suprasensory world, assume an air of intelligent superiority and consider you to be superstitious, as though saying, "You poor fool! We know that this is all pure nonsense." But then a Bjørnson or someone writes something in which spiritual matters play a role.* Something like this is then introduced into art, and everyone runs after it and enjoys a kind of knowledge in the arts that was otherwise rejected. Superstition can appear in strange guises.

I once had an acquaintance who was a dramatist. (Concrete examples should certainly be included when speaking of the art of education, which can be learned only from life.) One time I met him in the street; he was running very quickly and perspiring. It was three minutes before eight o'clock in the evening. I asked him where he was going in such a hurry. In his hurry, he could only say that he must rush to the post office, which closed at eight o'clock. I did not detain him, but psychologically I was interested in the reason for his haste, so I waited until he returned. After a while, he came back in a great heat, and he was more talkative. I asked him why he was in such a hurry to catch the post, and he said, "I have just sent off my play." He had always said that this play was not yet finished, and he said the same thing now: "It's true that the play is still unfinished, but I especially wanted to send it off today, so that the director would receive it

---

* Bjørnstjerne Bjørnson (1832–1910), Norwegian writer, editor, and theater director, known, with Henrik Ibsen, Alexander Kielland, and Jonas Lie, as one of the "four great ones" of nineteenth-century Norwegian literature. He was awarded the Nobel Prize for Literature in 1903.

tomorrow. I just wrote him a letter to say as much and asked him to be sure to send it back. You see, if a play is sent off before the end of the month, it may be chosen for a performance; otherwise there is no chance." This dramatist was an extremely enlightened and intelligent man. Nevertheless, he believed that if a play was despatched on a certain day it might be accepted, even if it had to be returned because it was unfinished.

This incident shows you how things that people are likely to despise creep into some hole, from which they raise their heads at the very next opportunity. This is especially true of children. We think we have managed to rid them of something, but then there it is again, somewhere else. We must learn to watch for this. We must open our hearts when studying the human being, so that a true art of education can be established on our understanding of the human being. Only by going into details can we fathom all these issues.

As I was saying, today religion, art, and science are spoken of as though they were entirely unrelated. This was not the case in the ancient past of human evolution, when they were completely united. Then, there were Mystery centers, which were also centers for education and culture, centers dedicated to the cultivation of religion, art, and science. Knowledge, then, was presented in pictures and mental images of the spirit world. They were received in an intuitive and comprehensive way that transformed them into outer, physical symbols, and these formed the basis of ceremonial cults. Science was embodied in those cults, as was art. Anything taken from the realm of knowledge and given outer form must be beautiful. Thus, in those times divine truth, a moral goodness, and a sensory perceptible beauty existed in the Mystery centers as a unity of religion, art, and science. Only later did this unity split to became science, religion, and art, each existing in and of itself.

Today, this separation has reached its culmination. Things that are essentially united have become divided through the course of cultural development. Human nature is such, however, that for us it is a necessity to experience the three as a unity and not see them as separate. People can experience the unity of religious science, scientific religion, and artistic ideality; otherwise, they are inwardly torn apart. Consequently, wherever this differentiation has become most intense, it is imperative to rediscover the connection between these three areas. And we will see in our teaching how we can bring art, religion, and science to children as a unity. We will see how children respond in a living way to this unification of religion, art, and science, because they are in harmony with their own inner nature. This is why I have repeatedly pointed out, in no uncertain terms, that we must work to educate children through the knowledge that they are in fact beings with aesthetic potential; we should neglect no opportunity to demonstrate how, during their first years, children experience religion naturally and instinctively.

All these things, the harmonious unification of religion, art, and science must be understood in the right way and their value recognized in the teaching methods that we will discuss further.

8 | Art & Language in Education

July 24, 1924

You can see by now that anthropo-sophic education truly values the fact that teachers must consciously know the whole human being. Various examples have shown that the typical worldview today is not at all capable of a deep understanding of the human being. Let me clarify what I mean. When we study the human being, we distinguish between the various constituent members. First, there is the physical body. Then we come to the finer ether body (or life body), which includes the formative forces of growth and the processes of nourishment, and which, during the early years of childhood, are transformed into the forces of memory. Then we add something that plants do not possess, though they, too, contain forces of growth and nourishment—and even memory—insofar as they maintain and repeat their forms. The next member is one that human beings have in common with animals, the sentient body, or astral body, which is the bearer of sensations. Added to this is the I organization. These four members must be distinguished, and to the degree that we do this, we can truly understand the human being and human evolution.

To begin with, our *initial* physical body, so to speak, arises from our heredity. This is prepared for us by our fathers and mothers. During the first seven years of life, that physical body is cast off, but during this time it is the model used by the ether body to build the second body. Today, people tend to oversimplify everything. If a boy of ten has a nose like his father's, people will say it is inherited. But it is not that simple; as a matter of fact, the nose is inherited, but only before the change of teeth. And if the ether body is strong enough to reject the model of the inherited nose, then it will change during the first seven years. On the other hand, if the ether body is weak, it will not be able to free itself from the model, and at the age of ten the shape of the nose will still be the same.

Externally, it seems as though heredity might still play the same role in the second seven-year period that it did during the first seven years. Here, people are likely to say that the truth must surely be simple. In reality, matters are more complicated. Today's views are mostly the result of laziness rather than an urgent desire for the truth. It is therefore very important that we learn to look with understanding at the body of formative forces, or ether body, which during the first seven years gradually creates the second physical body, which in turn also lasts about seven years. The ether body therefore creates form, or sculpts. Now, a true sculptor works independently and has no need for a model, whereas a poor sculptor makes everything according to a model. Likewise, during the first period of life and working toward the second, the ether body fashions the human being's second physical body.

Today's intellectual climate enables us to gain knowledge of the physical body; it serves this purpose well, and those who lack intellect cannot gain such knowledge. But our universities cannot go beyond this. The ether body cannot be understood intellectually, but only through the imagery of intuitive perception. It would have great significance if teachers could come to understand the ether body. One should not use the excuse that teachers cannot all be expected to develop clairvoyance to describe the ether body. But teachers could practice sculpture instead of studying the usual university courses. Those who truly work at sculpture and go into its formative qualities learn to experience the inner structure of forms, especially the kinds of forms that the human body of formative forces also work on.

Those who have a healthy sense of form experience the sculptural element only in the realm of animals and human beings, not those of the plant world. Just imagine a sculptor who wants to portray plants through sculpture. It would make you angry enough to strike such a person. A plant has a physical and an ether body, which make it complete. Animals, on the other hand, envelop an ether body with the astral body, and this is even more true of human beings. This is why we can begin to understand the human ether body by working as sculptors and entering the inner structure of natural forms. This, too, is why modeling should assume an important place in the a teachers' college curriculum, because it provides a way for teachers to understand the body of formative forces.

It is a fundamental principle that, if teachers have not studied modeling, they cannot truly understand child development. The art of education based on knowing the human being brings a heavy responsibility, because it points to such facts and brings with it corresponding requirements. It can also cause apprehension, because it seems as though you have to become extremely critical, rejecting every common practice.

Just as the ether body works to free itself and become independent at the change of teeth, so the astral body works toward independence at puberty. While ether body is a sculptor, the astral body is a "musician"; its structure is of the very essence of music. All that arises from the human astral body and becomes form is purely musical in nature. Those who can grasp this notion know that, to understand the human being, another level of training is required to become receptive to an inner musical world-view. Those who are not naturally musical cannot understand anything about the formation of the human astral body, because it is made of music. Thus, if we study the ancient periods of culture that were established on an inner musical intuition, and if we enter the Eastern periods of culture in which even language was imbued with music, then we find a musical view of the world even in their architectural forms. Later, in Greece, this changed, and now, especially in the West, it has changed radically; we have entered an age in which technology and mathematics are emphasized. At the Goetheanum in Dornach, we attempted to go backward in this sense. Musicians have sensed the music behind the forms of the Goetheanum. But, in general, this is poorly understood today.

Therefore, we need to gain a concrete understanding of the human being and gain the capacity to grasp the fact that the human physiological and anatomical form is a musical creation, insofar as it arises from the astral body. Look at the intimate connection between the musical element and the processes of breathing and blood circulation; human beings are musical instruments in the sense of breath and blood circulation. Consider the relationship between breathing and blood circulation: with eighteen breaths per minute and seventy-two heartbeats per minute, we get a ratio of four to one. Naturally, this varies in many ways, but by and large you find that the human being has an inner musical structure. The ratio of four to one has an inner rhythmic relationship itself and expresses something that impinges on and affects the whole organization in which human beings live and experience their own being. In ancient times, the meter of verses was established according to the breath and the metrical foot by the circulation. "Dactylus, dactylus, Caesar, dactylus, dactylus." Four in one, the line expressive of the human being.[*]

But what we express in language is expressed even earlier in this form. If you understand the human being from a musical perspective, you know that tones function within us. On our backs, where the shoulder blades meet and, from there, carried into our whole being, forming and shaping us, are the human forms constituted from the fundamental note of the scale. The form of the upper

---

[*] The metrical "foot" in the classical languages was based on the length of time taken to pronounce the syllables, categorized as long or short. The foot is often compared to a musical measure, the long and short syllables to whole and half notes. In English poetry, feet are determined by emphasis rather than length, with stressed and unstressed syllables serving the same function as long and short syllables in classical meter. A "dactyl" is a stressed syllable followed by two unstressed syllables: for example, "Canada," "holiday," "camouflage." The term comes from the Greek for "finger," and one can remember the pattern by thinking of the three joints in a finger: long, short, short.

arm corresponds with the second, and the lower arm with the third. And because there is a major and minor third (not a major and minor second), we have only one bone in the upper arm, but two in the lower arm, the radius and the ulna. These correspond to the major and minor third. We are formed according to the notes of the musical scale, the intervals hidden within us.

If you study the human being only in an external way, you cannot understand that the human form is made up of musical tones. With the hand, then, we have the fourth and fifth. In our experience of free movement, we go right out of ourselves, taking hold, as it were, of outer nature. This is the source of the feeling we have in response to the sixth and seventh, a feeling that is enhanced by experiencing eurythmy movements. Keep in mind that the use of the third appeared relatively late in the development of music. The experience of the third is inner; with the third, we realize an inner relationship with ourselves. When humankind lived in the seventh, however, people mostly experienced going out into the world outside themselves. The experience of surrender to the outer world lives with special strength in the seventh.

Just as we experience the inherent nature of music, so the forms of the human body are shaped from music. Thus, if teachers want to teach music well, they must make a point of getting children to sing from the very beginning of their years at school. This must be done, because the very act of singing induces freedom. The astral body already sang and released the forms of the human body. And between the change of teeth and puberty, the astral body frees itself. Out of the very essence of music, the forms that free human beings begin to emerge. No wonder, then, that when music teachers understand that we are thoroughly imbued with music they naturally allow this knowledge to enrich their singing and instrumental music lessons. This is why we not only introduce singing as early as possible into our education, but we also to allow children with the right aptitude to learn musical instruments, so that they can actually begin to grasp the musical element that lives in their human form as it emancipates itself.

None of this can be approached in the right way unless teachers have the right feeling for it. It ought to be clear that every teacher training college should be constituted so that its curriculum runs parallel to university level medical studies. The first approach leads to the kind of intellectual understanding that comes from studying anatomy; this should lead on to an artistic understanding of form, and this cannot be acquired unless, along with the study of physical anatomy, students practice modeling. Again, this should lead to an understanding of music. True knowledge of the human being cannot be attained unless medical studies are supplemented by an understanding of the role music plays in the world. During college training, student teachers should gain an understanding of music—not just externally but also inwardly—so that their inner perception sees music everywhere. Music is indeed everywhere in the world; one simply has to find it.

And, if you want to understand I being, you must master and make the inner nature and structure of some language your own. We understand the physical body through the intellect; the ether body through an understanding of form; the astral body through an understanding of music; and I being through of a deep and penetrating understanding of language. This is exactly where we are greatly lacking today, for there is a much we do not know. Consider the German language, for example. In German, this object that rests quietly on top of the body—round, with eyes and nose to the front—is called *Kopf*, but in Italian, it is called *testa*. A dictionary tells us that the translation of *Kopf* is "*testa*," but this is purely external and superficial. It's not even true.

It is true, however, that if you have a feeling for the vowels and consonants in *Kopf*, you will experience the *o* as a definite form that could be drawn—as eurythmists know—as the rounded form to the front that becomes the nose and mouth. And if we can allow ourselves to experience it, this combination of sounds reveals everything that is given in the form of the head. So, if we want to express that form, we use the larynx and lungs and pronounce the sounds approximating to "k–o–pf." We can say that the head also contains something that enables us to speak to one another. We can share what we wish to make known—say, a will. If you want to describe the head, not as round form, but as a vehicle for information that clearly defines what we wish to communicate, then the very nature of language gives you a means of doing so.

When you say "*testa*," you name what communicates; when you say "*Kopf*," you name a rounded form. If Italians wanted to describe the round characteristic, they would have to say "*Kopf*"; likewise, if Germans want to express the aspect of communication, they would have to say "*testa*." Both Italians and Germans, however, have grown accustomed to expressing something different in language, since it is impossible to express completely different things with a single word. Consequently, we are not saying exactly the same thing with the words *testa* and *Kopf*. The languages are different, because their words express different meanings.

Now let us go into the way the members of a particular nation live with the language of their folk soul. The German way of living in language is formative. The German language is really one of sculptural contemplation. This happened in German because, in the evolution of speech in Central Europe, the Greek element is retained. When you study Italian and the Romance languages in general, you find their configuration is such that they are developed out of the soul's motor function; they are not contemplative. Italian was formed from inner dancing or singing, from the soul's participation in the whole bodily organism. We can see how the I is related to the essence of the folk soul; by studying the inner relationships and makeup of language, we learn how I being functions.

Teachers thus need to gain not only a feeling for music, but also an inner feeling of language, starting with the fact that modern languages have retained only the soul's feeling experiences in exclamations. For example, when we say *"etsch!"* in German, it's as though someone had slipped and fallen, and we want to express this along with the amusement it causes. With exclamations, language retains feeling. In other respects, language has become abstract, it hovers above things, no longer inside them. But language must again become living and real. We must learn to grapple with language; we must be able to experience I being going right through the sounds. Then we can feel the difference between saying *"Kopf,"* which gives us an immediate feeling for drawing the head's form, or saying *"testa,"* which gives us the feeling of wanting to dance. Teachers must develop particularly this sense for "feeling one's way into life's activities."

If teachers can become accustomed to viewing the physical and spirit together—for they are indeed one, as I have repeatedly said—and if they can continually increase their ability to do this, teachers will never be tempted to delve into intellectual abstractions but endeavor to keep all education between the change of teeth and puberty within the realm of imagery. When you are accustomed to thinking pictorially about real things, there is nothing more distasteful than someone who talks intellectually and in a roundabout way; this becomes an unpleasant experience.

When you are accustomed to seeing life as it actually happens, you wish to describe it only as it is, completely in the image of it. Say, for example, you want to reach an understanding with someone, but that person forms judgments purely on the basis of intellect, describing everything as beautiful or ugly or wonderful. Everything is one way or the other—and you feel in your soul as if your hair were being pulled out by the roots. This is especially unpleasant if you would really like to know what the other has experienced, but this individual really never describes it. For example, I might speak of someone I know who raises her knee very high when she walks, and this person immediately responds, "She walks well," or, "She has a good carriage." This tells us nothing about the woman, only about this person's ego. But this is not what we are after; we are looking for an objective description.

This is very difficult for people today. People tend not to describe things, but the way things affect them, as "beautiful" or "ugly." And this gradually affects even the formation of language. Instead of describing the face itself, people will say something like, "He sure looks terrible today."

Awareness of such things should be part of the deepest training of teachers, to get rid of the self and to come to grips with reality. If you succeed in this, you will also be able to establish a real relationship with the children. Children feel just as I have described—that their hair is being pulled out by the roots when teachers do not get to the point, but speak only about their own feelings. If you simply stick with what is concrete and real and describe it, children will quickly get into it. So it is very important for teachers not to "overthink." I always feel it is a real problem when Waldorf teachers think too much, but it gives real satisfaction to see them develop a faculty for seeing even the smallest details and discovering their special qualities. If someone were to say to me, "This morning I saw a lady who was wearing a violet dress; it was cut in such and such a fashion, and her shoes had high heels," and so on, I would like it better than if some-one were to come and say, "The human being consists of physical body, ether body, astral body, and I being." The first is standing firmly within life with a developed ether body; the other has knowledge of the ether body, but it is merely intellectual and doesn't mean much.

I have to speak drastically so that we can recognize what is most important in a teacher's training. We should learn not to spin thoughts on things, but learn to observe life. We should learn to use such observations in life as matter of fact. We ruin everything, however, by racking our brains over how we might use it. This is why those who wish to describe something from spiritual science should strongly avoid the usual abstract concepts, because this moves away from what really wants to be said. And it is especially true that those who try to under-stand things in a usual way will tend toward generalities, not sharp definitions. Here is an extreme example. To me it is unpleasant to say, "A pale man is standing there." It hurts. On the other hand, the statement begins to breathe with reality if I say, "The man standing there is pale." In other words, I do not give a description in stiff, ordinary concepts, but describe, using the ideas that enclose it.

You will find that children have a greater inner understanding of things when they are expressed in relative form instead of in bare nouns qualified by adjectives. Children prefer a gentle way of handling things. When I say to them, "A pale man is standing there," it's like hitting something with a hammer. But if I say, "The man standing there is pale," it's like a stroking movement of my hand. Children find it much easier to adapt to the world if things are presented in this second form rather than by a hitting quality. We must develop a certain fineness of feeling if we wish to become sculptors of language and to place it in the service of the art of education. It also adds to education as an art if we strive to master language so that we can articulate our words clearly when teaching a class, knowing how to emphasize what is important and passing lightly over the insignificant.

We place great value on these things, and the teachers' conferences repeatedly draw attention to the qualitative in teaching. If you truly study a class, you notice all sorts of things that can help. For example, suppose you have a class of twenty-eight boys and girls and want to give them something they can make their own, something that will enrich their inner life. It may be a little poem, even a great poem. So, you try to teach this poem to the class. Now you will find that, if you have them all recite together, even a third or half of the class, each child will speak and be able to say it. But if you test one or two of the students to see if they can say it by themselves, you will find that they cannot. It is not that you have overlooked these two or failed to notice that they were silent; they can say it very well in chorus with the others. The fact is, however, that a group spirit pervades and activates the class, and you can make use of this.

So if you really work with the whole class of children as a chorus, at first it seems as if this invokes comprehension more quickly. But one time I had to point out the shadow side of this procedure, and so I will now give you a secret. There are shadow sides in a Waldorf school. Gradually we find our way and discover that handling a class as a chorus and allowing the children to speak together goes quite well; but when this is overdone, if we work only with the class without considering the individuals, the result will be that no individual child will know anything.

We must consider the shadow side of all such things and be clear about how far we can go in handling the class as a chorus, for example, and to what extent we need to work with individual children separately. Theories are useless here. To say it is good to treat the class as a chorus, or to maintain that things should be done in this or that way never helps, because, in the complexities of life, what we should do one way might also, given other conditions, be done another way. The worst that we can do in education—which is art rather than science—is to give abstract directions based on definitions. Education should always consist of this: Teachers are guided in such a way that they enter with understanding into the development of one or another human being, and through the most convincing examples, are led to knowledge of the human being.

Method follows naturally if we work this way. Consider, for example, methods of teaching to children under nine or ten years; it is futile and closed to such young children. At nine or ten (you can observe this yourselves) they begin to be interested in individuals. You can portray Caesar, Achilles, Hector, Agamemnon, or Alcibiades simply as people, allowing historical context to become only a background. By painting a picture this way, the children will show real interest. It will be obvious that they are eager to know more. They feel an urge to go more into the lives of these historic figures if you describe them in this way. Comprehensive pictures of personalities, complete in themselves—pictures of how a meal looked during one century or another; pictorial descriptions of how people ate before forks were invented; how they generally ate meals in ancient Rome; descriptions of how a Greek walked, aware of each step and the leg's form; describing how the Hebrew people of the Old Testament walked, with no feeling for form, but slouching with their arms hanging loose—invoking feelings for these various and distinct images is the right approach to teaching history to children of ten to twelve years old.

Now, at this age, we can take another step and move on to historic relationships, because until now children are unable to understand concepts such as cause and effect. Only now can historic connections be presented in history, but everything historic be worked out in ways that show a gradual development. Here we come to the concept of growth, or becoming. You could invoke an image of how we are alive now in 1924. Charles the Great lived from 760 to 814, so using 800 as the approximate date, we find he lived 1,120 years ago. We imagine ourselves living in the world as a child growing up, and we can assume that, in the course of a century, we would have a son or daughter, father and mother, grandfather and perhaps even a great-grandfather. In other words, we have maybe three or four generations, one after another in a hundred years. We can demonstrate these generations by having someone to stand and represent the son or daughter. The parent will stand behind that person with hands resting on the shoulders of the one in front; the grandfather will place his hands on the shoulders of the father, and the great-grandfather his hands on the shoulders of the grandfather. If you imagine son, father, and grandfather, one behind the other as people belonging to the present age, and behind them the generations over the course of ten centuries, you will need eleven times three or four generations, say forty-four generations. So, if you were to place forty-four people in this way, each with hands on the shoulders of the one in front, the first might be a man of today, and the last would be Charles the Great.

Thus you can change temporal relationships in history, which are so difficult to see, into visible spatial relationships. You could also picture it in another way. You have one person speaking to another; the second one turns and speaks a third one behind, who then does the same, and so it goes on until you are back to the time when Peter spoke to Christ. Thus, the whole development of the Christian church is shown by a conversation between people standing one behind the other. The whole apostolic succession is revealed visually.

Seize every opportunity to use images and tangible objects. This helps children find a way into the real world and to form everything in keeping with reality. It's simply arbitrary to place three beans before the children, add another three, and then yet another four, and then teach them addition: 3 + 3 + 4 = 10. This is quite arbitrary. But it is completely different if I have an unknown number of beans in a small pile; this is how things are in the world. When I divide the pile, the children will quickly understand this. I give some to one child, some to another, and another portion to a third child. I divide the pile, first showing them how many beans there are altogether. I begin with the total and go to the parts. The child could count the beans, since it is just a repetitive process—one, two, three, and so on, up to twelve. But I divide them into four, into four more, and again into another four. If I begin with the total and proceed to the parts, the children take it in more easily; it accords with reality. The other way is abstract—just putting things together intellectually. It is also more real if I get them to the point where they must answer a question: If I have twelve apples, and someone takes them and returns only seven, how many have I lost? Here we begin with the minuend, then go from the remainder to the subtrahend; we do not subtract, but go from the remainder, or from what remains as the result of a living process, to what has been taken away.

Thus our efforts are not always directed toward abstractions; they find an outlet in reality, and being linked to life, they strive after life. This affects the children and makes them bright and lively, whereas teaching arithmetic has a largely deadening effect. The children remain "dead" and apathetic, and the inevitable result of this is the calculator. The very fact that we have calculators proves how difficult it is to make arithmetic available to perception. But we must not do this alone; we must learn to read from life itself.

9 | Renewing Education

July 24, 1924, Afternoon

*I*t can truly be said that the accomplishments of our schools become a part of the whole culture and development of civilization. It does this either in a more direct way so that we can easily see it in the way a civilization is expressed in its art of education, or it may go unnoticed. Civilization always reflects the nature of its schools, but this often goes unobserved. We will describe this through the example of our own era, but first we will discuss Eastern culture.

We really know very little about the more ancient Eastern culture and what remains of it. Eastern culture has absolutely no intellectual aspect but arises directly from the human being as a whole—in an Eastern form—and its goal is to unite human beings. It rises above the principle of authority only with great difficulty, and its forms tend to arise from love in a natural way. We cannot speak of a separate teacher and a separate student in the Eastern world, as we would in our culture. There you do not have the teacher but a "dada." The dada shows the way through personality and represents all that should imbue a growing human being. The dada is the one who *shows* everything and never teaches anything. It would make no sense to teach in Eastern culture. The educational views of Herbart, a well-known educational theorist in Europe, were widely accepted in Central Europe.* Herbart once stated that he could not imagine education without teaching. To him, everything revolved around what one thinks. The Eastern individual would not have been able to imagine an education based on teaching, because everything that should develop in students was presented through a living example. This is also true of the relationship between an initiate, or guru, and a chela, or disciple. The disciple is not taught but learns through example.

By going more deeply into this, you will understand this: All Waldorf education is directed toward the whole human being. Our purpose is not to separate spiritual and physical education, but when we educate the body, our education even affects illnesses and their ramifications. Our physical education employs fundamental spiritual principles, which are also very practical. Our purpose is to allow spirit to work actively within the body. Thus, in a Waldorf school, physical education is not neglected but developed from our knowledge that human beings are soul *and* spirit. In every way, our education involves everything needed to educate the body.

Furthermore, one must come to understand something that was understood by the ancient Greeks, whose education was based on gymnastics. The teachers were gymnasts, and they knew the meaning of human movement. In earlier Greek times, it would have been virtually incomprehensible to think that they should introduce children to logic. The Greeks understood the healthy results of teaching children gymnastics—in a milder form

---

* Johann Friedrich Herbart (1776–1841), philosopher and pedagogue.

in Athens, and in a more difficult and arduous way in Sparta. It was perfectly clear to them that, if they could use their fingers in a dexterous way when taking hold of something, the movement would flow into their whole organism, and through the agile use of their limbs, they could learn to think clearly. One also learns to speak well by performing gymnastic movements in the correct way.

Everything involved in inner spiritual training that tends toward abstraction develops unnaturally through direct instruction. This sort of training should arise from the way we learn to move our bodies—and this is why our civilization has become so abstract. Today there are those who cannot sew on a button. In Waldorf schools, the boys and girls are together and the boys become enthusiastic about knitting and crocheting; through this they also learn to manipulate their thoughts. It is not surprising that people, regardless of their training in logical thinking, cannot think clearly if they are incapable of knitting. We can see that the thinking of today's women is much more flexible. One merely needs to look at the results of admitting women to universities to see how much more flexible the soul of women is than that of men, who have become stiff and abstract through activities that lead away from reality. We see this in its worst form in the business world. Seeing how a man of business conducts his affairs can drive you crazy.

These things must be understood again today. Teachers must know that, no matter how much they draw on the blackboard or provide intellectual explanations, children will learn to tell the difference between acute and obtuse angles and come to understand the world much better, if they practice holding a pencil between their toes, for example, to make reasonably formed angles and letters—

in other words, when human spirit flows from the whole body. Greek culture carefully taught children how to move, to endure heat and cold, and to adapt to the physical world, because there was a feeling that soul and spirit develop correctly from a properly developed physical body. Greeks were educated as gymnasts; they grasped and mastered the whole person; the outer faculties were allowed to develop from such mastery.

Because of modern scientific thinking, we are aware of an important fact, but we understand it in only an abstract way. When children are quick to learn how to write with the right hand, we know that this is related to the human center of speech in the left hemisphere of the brain. We see a connection between hand movement and speech. Similarly, through physiology we can understand the relationship between movement and thinking. So today we already know—though in a somewhat abstract way—how thinking and speaking arise from the human faculty of movement; but the Greeks knew this in a most comprehensive sense. Gymnasts knew people learn to think in a coordinated way by learning to skillfully walk, jump, and throw a discus. When one learns to throw the discus beyond the goal, one can comprehend the logic behind the story of Achilles and the tortoise; one learns to grasp the remarkable forms of logic that the Greeks described. In this way, one learns to stand firm in reality.

Today we generally think something along these lines: Here is a lawyer and there is the client; the lawyer knows things that the client does not. In Greece, however, because it was usual to throw the discus beyond the mark, the Greeks understood something like this: Here is an educated lawyer with a student whom he instructs in legal matters. The student learned so well that he can never lose a lawsuit. But what would happen if a lawsuit involved both student and teacher? The student would always win and always lose; of course, the case would be left hanging in the air. Thus, thinking and speaking developed from an education based on gymnastics; both were drawn from the whole human being.

Now consider the Roman civilization, in which the whole person receded into the background, though something remained in the *mannerism* of the Roman. Greek movement was alive, pristine, and natural. The Romans in their togas looked very different from the Greeks; they also moved differently, because their movement had become a mannerism. In place of movement, education was directed toward only a part of the human being; it was based on beautiful speech. This was still very significant, because in speech the whole upper part of the body is engaged, right down into the diaphragm and bowels. A considerable part of a person is engaged while learning to speak with beauty. In education, every effort was made to approach the human being, to make something of the human being.

This was still true when culture passed into medieval times. In Greece, the most important educators were the gymnasts, who worked on the whole person; in the Roman civilization, the most important educators were the rhetoricians. In Greece, all culture and worldviews were based on human beauty, conceived as a whole. We cannot understand a Greek poem or statue if we do not know that the Greek's whole worldview was centered on the concept of the human being in movement. When we look at a Greek statue and see the movement of the mouth, we are led to wonder about the relationship between that movement and the position of the foot, and so on. It is completely different when we consider Roman art and culture. There, rhetoricians replaced the gymnasts, with the entire cultural life focused on oratory. All education was to train public speakers, to develop beautiful speech and eloquence. This continued right into the Middle Ages, when education still worked on the human being. You can see the truth of this by understanding the substance and goals of education during the Middle Ages. They had the seven liberal arts, for example—grammar, rhetoric, dialectic, arithmetic, geometry, astronomy (or astrology), and music.

Jesuit training was the cultural stream that carried this into later times and to the present. From the beginning and into the eighteenth century, its main purpose to train—even "drill"—human beings to develop a powerful will, and to place them as such into life. From the beginning, this was the aim of Jesuit culture. And it was only during the nineteenth century, to keep from falling behind others, that the Jesuits introduced the exact sciences into their teaching. Through these methods, the Jesuits developed strong, energetic characters—so much so that, even if you oppose Jesuitism, you have to wonder whether human beings could be trained to work today with such purpose for the good, as the Jesuits have trained people to work for the decadence of humankind.

Arithmetic was not practiced as it is today; it was taught in order to develop a capacity of working with form and number. The study of music enabled students to gain a deeper experience of life as a whole. And astronomy helped students develop a capacity for cosmic thinking. All these studies approached the human being directly. Today's "exact" sciences played a negligible part in education. The idea that students should *understand* science was considered of little value. It was much more important to be able to move and speak well and to think and calculate. The acquisition of readymade truth was less important. Hence the whole perspective of civilization developed in order to produce people who could play a role in public life and willingly to devote themselves to this. One was proud of those who could hold their own as public orators and who were thoroughly representative individuals.

This trend in human development first appeared in the Roman civilization, when rhetoricians emerged from the gymnasts. In a civilization based on rhetorical education, we see the tremendous value placed on everything significant in the area of speech. Now try to look back at life as a whole during the Middle Ages, when everything was viewed from the perspective of rhetoric, and this gets into matters such as how to act, how to greet one another, and so on. All this is not taken for granted, but practiced according to a concept of beauty, just as, in rhetoric, one derives aesthetic pleasure from a way of speaking that conforms to a concept of beauty. Here you see the growing overall importance of an education in rhetoric, whereas the whole significance of a Greek education is based on expression through human movement.

In the sixteenth century, we come to a more modern period, though in fact we see some preparation for this in the fifteenth century. Again, something that represented much in the human being—in this case, rhetoric—is pushed to the background. Just as rhetoric had pushed back gymnastic training, now rhetoric is pushed back and limited, leading to an ever increasing effort toward intellectuality. Just as Roman educators were rhetoricians, our educators are doctors and professors. Gymnasts were complete human beings, and rhetoricians appeared in public wanting to represent human beings, but our professors have ceased to be human at all. They deny the human being and live increasingly through sheer abstractions; they are now merely skeletons of civilization.

Today, professors dress like anyone else; they no longer like to wear caps and gowns in the lecture halls, but dress in such a way that it is not immediately obvious that they are merely skeletons of civilization. Ever since the sixteenth century, our entire education has focused on the professor. And those who educate in terms of what is important in the world no longer bring to the schools any understanding of human development and training, but merely impart facts to the children. Children are expected to absorb knowledge; real development is ignored, but they are expected to gain knowledge and acquire learning. Those in favor of educational reform certainly complain loudly enough about this academic attitude, but they cannot escape it. There are those who are fully aware of such matters and have a clear image of the way Greek children were educated. They see what happens in modern schools where, although gymnastics are taught, human development and training of the whole being is completely ignored, and scraps of scientific knowledge are instead given to the youngest children. And they see that it is not just the teachers who have become skeletons of civilization—or at least consider this an ideal or essential requirement—but now the little children also look as though they were mini-professors. And if we wish to express the difference between a Greek child and a modern child, one could say that Greek child was human, and a modern child easily becomes a small professor.

This is the major change in the world in terms of the formation and development of culture: we no longer look at the human being, but only at what can we can present as facts that people can know and hold on to as information. Western civilization has developed downward to the point where gymnasts have descended to rhetoricians, and rhetoricians to professors. We must discover the upward direction again. The most important words for modern education are these: *Professors must be replaced with something new.* We must again turn our attention to the whole human being.

Consider how this is expressed in the global significance of education. In Central Europe recently, there was a university with a professor of eloquence (or rhetoric). If we look back to the early nineteenth century, we find these professors of eloquence in many places of learning; this was all that remained of the old rhetoric. At the university I am thinking of, there was a truly important person who was considered a professor of eloquence. But he would never have gotten anyone to listen to him if he had limited himself to this, because people no longer had the least interest in listening to eloquence. He lectured instead on Greek archeology. In the university register, he was listed as "professor of eloquence," but in fact one would hear only his lectures on Greek archeology. He had to teach something that leads to knowledge, not to a *capacity.* And indeed this has become the ideal of modern teaching. It leads to a life in which people know a tremendous amount. In a world where people know so much, it hardly seems earthly any more.

People have much knowledge and little ability; the function is lacking that leads from knowledge to capacity. For example, you may study for the medical profession, and then comes the time for final examinations. You are told, officially, that you cannot do anything yet; you must now go through years of internship. But it is absurd that students are not taught during their first years so that they can do something from the beginning. Why would children learn to do arithmetic if they could only add? What is the purpose of knowing about a town if you know only what it looks like? Wherever we go, the point is to enter life. Professors lead away from life, not into it.

An example shows us the significance of education in the world. When people attended the Olympic games in Greece, it was still apparent what the Greeks valued so much; they recognized that only gymnasts could be schoolteachers. It was similar during the time of rhetoricians. And what about now? There are those who would like to bring the Olympic games back to life, but this is merely a whimsey, since people no longer need them. They merely imitate those games superficially, and nothing can be gained by this. Something else penetrates right into human beings today. It is centered neither in our speech, nor in our studied bearing and gestures, but is centered in thinking. Consequently, the significance that science has for the world today is demonic. This demonic quality arises from the popular belief that intellectual thinking furthers cultural development; life is supposed to be shaped by theories. This is true of modern socialism, for example, whose whole tenor shapes life according to concepts. Marxism entered the world through a few clumsy, preconceived ideas such as "surplus value" and the like, which were intended to form the basis for determining and ordering life. Nobody saw the real connections and consequences, but research into the whole is an absolute necessity.

Consider a more westerly part of Central Europe. Decades ago, there was a philosopher there whose teaching no longer contained anything living. He turned everything into concepts, believing that life could be formed conceptually. And he presented these beliefs in his lectures. He preferred Russian students, and he had many; his philosophy eventually took the form of bolshevism. He himself remained an ordinary, upstanding, middle-class citizen. At the time, he had no idea what he was doing by sowing the seed of his philosophy. Out of it grew the remarkable blossom of bolshevism. The seed of bolshevism was first sown in the universities of the West; it was sown in thoughts and in the abstract, intellectual education of a rising generation. One who knows nothing about plants has no idea what will sprout from a seed; likewise, people had no idea what would grow from the seed they planted. They failed to see the consequences until the seed had begun to grow, because people no longer understand life's great interrelationships.

The real significance of modern intellectual education in the world is that it leads away from life. We see this by looking at certain external matters. We had books before the World War. Of course, one masters their content only by reading them or by making notes. Otherwise they remain in the library, which is a cultural coffin. But when someone needs to produce a thesis, the books must be checked out. This happens in an external way, and one is happy if their content enters only the head and no further. This is the way things are everywhere.

Now look at life. We have an economy, a legal system, and our culture. They all function, but think little about it. We no longer think about inner realities, but only about the balance sheet. What is the real concern of banking for our economy—or even our culture, when, for example, the accounts of schools are prepared? These contain the abstract figures of balance sheets. And what have these figures brought about in life? People are no longer personally connected to what they do. People have gradually reached the point where it makes no difference whether they are grain merchants or haberdashers; a pair of pants means as much as anything else. One merely calculates the profits of the business, searching through abstract figures with an eye for what might prove more lucrative.

Banks have replaced the living economy. People draw money out of the banks, but apart from that, banking is left to economic abstractions. Everything has been changed into superficial abstractions, with the result that no one is involved in a human way. When banks were first established, it was closely connected to human beings, because people were used to living within the real work of existence, as was true in earlier times. Even during the first half of the nineteenth century, this was still true. Bank directors still gave it a personal character; they were actively engaged in it with their will; they lived with it as personalities. In this connection, I would like to relate a story that describes how the banker Rothschild behaved when the king of France sent a representative to arrange state credit. When the ambassador arrived, Rothschild was consulting with a leather dealer. The ambassador, who was concerned with arranging credit, was properly announced. Rothschild, whose business with the leather dealer had not finished, sent a message asking the ambassador to wait. The minister could not understand how an ambassador from the king of France could possibly be kept waiting, and he asked to be announced again. Rothschild replied that he was engaged in business concerning leather, not with state affairs. The minister became so angry that he burst into Rothschild's room, exclaiming, "I am the ambassador for the king of France!" Rothschild replied, "Please take a chair." The ambassador, thinking he had not heard correctly, could not conceive that someone in his position would be offered a chair. He repeated, "I am the ambassador for the king of France!" But Rothschild merely replied, "Take two chairs, then."

We see how the personality still made itself felt in those days, because it was still present. What about today? Personality is present in exceptional cases, for example, when someone breaks through as a public official. Otherwise, where there was once a personality, now there is a joint stock company. There is no human personality at the center of things. If we ask what a joint stock company is, the answer may be that it is a society of people who are wealthy today and poor tomorrow. Such matters follow a very different course today than they did in earlier times—today wealth piles up, tomorrow it dissolves. People are cast here and there in these fluctuations, and money carries on its own business. Today, people are delighted when they come into a great deal of money. They buy a car, then buy another one. Things go on like this until the situation changes and money becomes scarce. One is forced to sell one of the cars and then the other. This points to the fact that people are no longer in control of the economy and business. People have been removed from the objective course of business life.

I presented this for the first time in 1908 in Nuremberg, but people understood little about it. It was the same during the spring of 1914, when I said in Vienna that everything is headed toward a great world catastrophe. Human beings are no longer included in concrete reality;

they are becoming more and more a part of the abstract, and it is obvious that abstraction inevitably leads to chaos. But people could not understand this.*

Now, above all else, if we have a heart for education, we must bear in mind that we have to free ourselves from abstraction and work our way back to concrete reality, realizing that everything depends on the human being. We should not emphasize too strongly the need for teachers who have a thorough knowledge of geography, history, English, or French; rather, teachers must understand the human being. Teachers should build their teaching on the basis of real knowledge of the human being. Then, if necessary, they can sit and look in an encyclopedia for the material they need for teaching. If people do this, while standing firmly on the ground of a real understanding and knowledge of the human being, as teachers they will teach better than those who have excellent degrees but lack real knowledge of the human being.

Thus we come to the meaning of an art of education in the world. We know that what happens in the school is reflected in the culture of the outer world. This was easy to see in the case of the ancient Greeks. Gymnasts were seen everywhere in public life. When Greeks stood before the agora, or marketplace, regardless of what they were like in other ways, it was obvious that they were educated as gymnasts. In the case of Romans, their training manifested less externally. And with us, what lives in the school is expressed by the fact that life increasingly escapes us; we grow *out* of life, no longer into it. We have

---

* Nuremberg: *The Apocalypse of St. John: Lectures on the Book of Revelation*, London: Rudolf Steiner Press, 1993; 12 lectures, June 17–30, 1908. Vienna: *The Inner Nature of Man and Our Life Between Death and Rebirth*, London: Rudolf Steiner Press, 1994; 8 lectures, April 6–14, 1914.

no idea of the degree to which our accounting systems lead their own independent life—life so removed that we have lost all power over it. It takes its own course, leading an abstract existence based on numbers. Just consider those who are highly educated. At best, we recognize them because they wear glasses (or perhaps not) on their attenuated little organ. Education today has significance only because it is gradually undermining the significance of the larger world.

We must bring the world, the real world, back into the schools. Teachers must stand within this world, with a lively interest in everything in the world. Only when teachers are "of the world" can the world be brought into the schools in a living way. The world must live within the schools. Even if this happens only playfully at first, then in an aesthetic way, and gradually finding expression, it is nonetheless imperative that the world lives in the school. So today it is more important than ever to emphasize this approach of mind and heart in our new education and to be rethinking our methods. Many of the older methods are still good, and what I have been saying is certainly not meant to cast a shadow over the excellent educators of the nineteenth century. I appreciate them fully; in fact, I see those nineteenth-century teachers as people of genius and great capacity, but they were the children of an intellectual time; they used their capacity to work toward the intellectualizing of our age. People today have no idea how much they have been imbued with intellectuality.

Here we come to the real significance of renewed education—that we free ourselves from intellectuality. The various branches of human life will be able to reunite. People will understand what it means when education was seen as a means of healing, which was connected with the significance of human beings. There was a time when the idea, or image, of the human being was this: When we were born into earthly existence, we were actually a stage below human; we had to be educated and healed in order to rise and become truly human. Education was therapeutic and a part of medicine and hygiene. Today everything is divided. Teachers are placed along side the school doctor, outwardly separate. But this just doesn't work. To place teachers side by side with the school doctor is like looking for a tailor who makes the left side of a coat, and for another who makes the right side, with no idea about who might sew the two parts together. Likewise, if we take the measurements of teachers, who are not trained in medicine (the right side of the coat), and then take the measurements of the doctor, who was not trained in education (the left side), who will sew them together? We must actively rid ourselves of the "left" and "right" tailors and replace them with one who can make a whole coat. Impossible situations seldom appear unless life has been greatly limited, not when life is springing up and bubbling over.

This is why it is so difficult for people to understand the meaning of Waldorf education. Sectarian efforts away from life is the opposite of what it intends. On the contrary, it works intensively to enter life.

In such a short lecture course, it is clearly possible to give only a short overview of everything involved. I have attempted to do this, and I hope it may have been stimulating. I will conclude our course in the final lecture.

10 | Education & the Anthroposophic Movement

July 24, 1924, Afternoon[*]

*B*ecause I am coming to the conclusion of this lecture course on education, I would like to express my deep satisfaction that our friends in Holland have assumed the task of nurturing anthroposophy and have taken the initiative to arrange this course. Such enterprises always involve a great deal of hard work for the organizers. And, because we have so much to arrange in Dornach, we know very well what goes on behind the scenes of such occasions. There is much work to do, which calls for a tremendous effort and energy. So, before leaving Holland, it is clear that I must express my very warmest thanks to those who have worked together to bring this whole conference to fruition. An educational course has taken place, and in my closing words I may be permitted to say something about the role of the art of education within the whole realm of the anthroposophic movement.

An educational art has grown within the anthroposophic movement—not as something that found its way into the movement through abstract intentions, but

---

* This concluding talk took place immediately after the previous lecture.

through necessity and the movement itself. Until now, few activities have arisen as naturally and inevitably from the anthroposophic movement as has this art of education. Likewise, as a matter of course, eurythmy has grown from the anthroposophic movement through Marie Steiner, and medicine through Dr. Wegman. And, as with the other two, educational art has, I venture to say, arisen likewise according to destiny. The anthroposophic movement is, without doubt, an expression that corresponds to human efforts that result from the very fact that humanity has come about on earth.

Just recall the ancient times when the various Mystery centers cultivated religion, art, and science through spiritual experience. It makes us realize how, in those ancient, sacred centers, human beings conversed with suprasensory beings to bring the life of spirit into outer, physical life. We can find our way further into the history of human development and discover again and again the urge to add suprasensory reality to the sensory reality of humankind. These perspectives open when we penetrate the history of human evolution; we see that, within anthroposophy today, there is ceaseless human effort. Anthroposophy lives out of the longings and endeavours of human souls living today. And it may be said in truth that, at the turn of the nineteenth and twentieth centuries, it became possible for those who have the will to receive revelations from the spirit world, and these will again deepen the whole worldview of humankind.

Today, revelations from the spirit world must manifest in a way that differs from the old Mystery truths; they must accord with modern science, and these are the essence of anthroposophy. And those who make them their own also know that, out of the conditions of today, many more people would come to anthroposophy if it weren't for the tremendous amount of biased, preconceived feelings and ideas that block their path. But these things must be overcome. A larger circle of anthroposophists must grow from our small one. And if we imagine everything that lives and works in this group, without declaring anthroposophy a religious movement, we may allow a deeply moving picture to arise before us.

Imagine the Mystery of Golgotha. Only a hundred years later, the most brilliant Roman writer, Tacitus, wrote of Christ as though he were virtually unknown—someone who had met his death over in Asia. At the time, at the height of Roman civilization and culture, people were living the traditions of the previous several thousand years, and even then nothing was known of Christ. It is possible to paint a picture of an important fact with words: There above is Roman civilization—the arenas, the brilliant performances, and everything that takes place in Roman society and state government. Below are the underground areas known as the catacombs. Many people are gathered by the graves of those who, like themselves, believed in the Mystery of Golgotha. These people must keep everything secret. Their underground activities surface only when a Christian is smeared with pitch and burned in the arena as an entertainment for the civilized citizens. We have two worlds: Above is the life of Roman civilization, based on their ancient, resplendent traditions; below is a life developing secretly beneath the earth. Let us consider the brilliant writer of this period. He wrote what amounts to no more than a passing reference in his notes on the birth of Christianity, while his desk in Rome may have stood over the catacombs, and he had no idea what was taking place beneath him.

Several hundred years later, what had spread in such a spectacular way had disappeared; the Christian civilization has surfaced, and Christianity is expanding in Europe where there had been Roman culture before. Keeping this picture in view, we see the actual process of human evolution. Often, when people contemplate the present time, they are inclined to say that, certainly, anthroposophists do not hide under the earth today; this is no longer the custom, nor would they have to do so. In an outward sense, anthroposophists find themselves in surroundings as beautiful as any. But ask yourselves whether those who lay claim to ordinary civilization know any more about what happens here than did the Romans about what was happening in the catacombs.

We can no longer speak so precisely; the situation has become more intellectual, but it also remains the same. If we look forward a few hundred years in our thinking, we may indulge the courageous hope that this picture will change. And, of course, those who are as ignorant of anthroposophy as the Romans were about Christianity will find this to be a fantasy, but you cannot work actively in the world if you are unable to look courageously at the path before you. And anthroposophists gladly look with such courage at the path ahead. This is why such pictures arise in the mind's eye.

Occasionally, we must look at the various opinions about anthroposophy. It has gradually come about that hardly a week goes by without the publication of some antagonistic book on anthroposophy. Opponents seem to take anthroposophy very seriously. They refute it almost every week—not so much from the perspective different views, because they are not that inventive, but they do deny it. It is interesting to see how anthroposophy is dealt

with in this way. We discover that otherwise very educated people (or those who should have some sense of
responsibility) write books on some subject and introduce
what they have read about anthroposophy. Often they
have not read a single book by an anthroposophic author,
but gather information from the works of opponents.

Consider this example: At one time, there were Gnostics, of which little remains except the Pistis Sophia, a
writing that contains very little and is very difficult to
understand. Today, there are those who write about the
Gnostics (it seems very popular), and though they know
very little about it, they consider themselves its expo-
nents. They think it is correct to say that Gnosticism arose
from Greek culture. I often wonder what it would be like
if anthroposophy were treated this way—if, as many frequently wish, all its spiritual scientific writings were lost
to fire. Anthroposophy would become known just as the
Gnostics are known today. It is interesting that people
often say that anthroposophy is just warmed-over Gnosticism. They do not understand anthroposophy, because
they have no wish to know it, and they do not know the
Gnostics, because no physical documentation exists.[*]
Nevertheless this is how people talk. It is negative but
indicates a particular problem. Courage and strength will
be needed to prevent anthroposophy going the way of
Gnosticism; it must be developed so that it manifests its
intrinsic reality. If we truly face such matters, we are
deeply satisfied by the various endeavors that arise—

---

[*] The Nag Hammadi texts, or so-called Gnostic Gospels, were discovered
in Egypt more than twenty years after these lectures. The so-called Dead
Sea Scrolls, also thought to have connections with the Gnostics, were discovered in eleven caves near Qumran and the Dead Sea, beginning
around 1947.

which this conference exemplifies. Such initiative, taken together, should insure that anthroposophy will continue to work powerfully in the future.

In this educational course, anthroposophy has peeked in through little windows. Much has been suggested, however, and this may show how anthroposophy goes hand in hand with reality, penetrating right into everyday life. And because everything real is imbued with spirit, we cannot know and understand reality unless we have an eye for the spirit. Of course, it was impossible to speak here about anthroposophy itself. On the other hand, it was quite possible to speak of an area of activity where anthroposophy can work fruitfully—in education.

In the case of eurythmy, for example, it was destiny that spoke. Today, looking at things from outside, it might be imagined that someone was struck by the sudden thought that we need eurythmy. But this was not the case. At the time, the father of a family had died. There were several children, and the mother was concerned about them. She was anxious that something worthwhile should come of them. The anthroposophic movement was still small. I was asked, "What could develop from those children?" It was this question that led to the first steps toward eurythmy. Our first attempts were narrowly limited, but from these circumstances the first sugges- tions for eurythmy were given. Destiny had spoken, and it manifested because anthroposophy exists, and some- one standing on anthroposophic ground was seeking her calling. Soon (it did not take long) the first students of eurythmy became teachers and were able to carry eurythmy into the world. So, with the help of Marie Steiner, who took it under her wing, eurythmy became what it is today. In such a case, we might not feel that eurythmy has been sought, but rather that eurythmy sought out anthroposophy.

Now consider medicine. Dr. Ita Wegman has been a member of the Anthroposophical Society since the beginning. Her first attempts to heal through artistic perception gave her a predisposition to work medically in the anthroposophic movement. As a devoted anthroposophist, she has dedicated herself to medicine, which has also grown from the being of anthroposophy. Today it remains firmly within it, because it grew through a particular person.

Once the waves of the World War subsided, people's thoughts turned in every direction. But, eventually, something great must happen. Because people have suffered so much, they need to find the courage to accomplish something great—a complete change of heart. Great ideals were the order of the day. Authors of all stripes who might have written on other subjects wrote about such matters as the future of the state or society. Everywhere, thoughts turned to what could now arise through human efforts. Out of the soil of spiritual science, many things sprang up and then faded away. In the realm of education, there was little to show until now. My little book, *The Education of the Child*, appeared more or less at the beginning of the anthroposophic movement. It contained many suggestions that could be developed into a whole system of education. But it was not considered special— merely a booklet that might help mothers raise their children. I was always asked whether a child should be dressed, say, in blue or in red. Should this child be given a yellow bed-cover, or that child a red one? I was asked what a child should eat, and so on. This was admirable in terms of education, but it did not amount to much.

Then in Stuttgart, out of all these confused ideals, Emil Molt's idea emerged to establish a school for the children of the workers at the Waldorf Astoria Cigarette Factory. And Emil Molt—who is here today—had the idea of giving me the responsibility for directing the school. This was a foregone conclusion; destiny would not have allowed otherwise. The school was established with a hundred and fifty children of the factory workers, and staffed by teachers drawn from the anthroposophic movement. Wurtemberg school regulations allowed us to choose men and women we deemed suitable to teach. The only condition was that the prospective teachers should be able to prove in a general way that they were suited to the task. All this happened before the great "freeing of humanity" that occurred through the Weimar National Assembly. After that, we would never have been able to proceed so freely. As it was, we were able to begin, and it will be possible at least for a few years to maintain the lower classes also.*

Anthroposophy took over the school—or perhaps the school took over anthroposophy. In a few years the school grew and children were coming from diverse backgrounds and classes. All kinds of people wanted their children to attend the Waldorf school, regardless of whether they were anthroposophists. Very strange opinions arose. Of course, parents are fondest of their own children and want them to attend an excellent school. For example, there are many opponents whose hostility is based on science; they know that anthroposophy is merely a collection of foolish and unscientific rubbish. Nevertheless, they are willing to send their children to a

---

* A state law might prevent children from entering the school before the fifth grade.

Waldorf school. They even realize that Waldorf education suits their children very well.

Recently two such people visited the school and said, "This Waldorf school is really good; we can see this in our children. But what a pity that it's based on anthroposophy." Of course, the school would not have come about at all if not for anthroposophy. As you can see, the judgment of many people amounts to saying: There is an excellent dancer; it's a pity he has to stand on two legs. This is the logic of our opponents. We can only say that the Waldorf school is good; nothing in the school is planned so that it promotes any particular worldview. In terms of religious instruction, the Catholic children are taught by a Catholic priest, the evangelical children by an evangelical minister; and because there are so many in Germany who belong to no religious community, we had to arrange for a "free religion" class. Otherwise those children would have had no religious teaching at all.

I find it difficult to find teachers for the free religion lessons, because the classes are so full. We never try to persuade children to attend, since we want to be a modern school. We simply hope to have practical and fundamental principles for instruction. Nor do we have any desire to introduce anthroposophy to the school, because we are not a sect. We are concerned only with matters that are universally human. Nevertheless, we cannot prevent children from leaving the evangelical or Catholic religion lessons and attending the free religion lesson. We cannot be blamed if they come. But we are responsible for making sure that the free religion lessons continue.

Little by little, the Waldorf school is growing. There are now about eight hundred children and between forty and fifty teachers. Its growth is well in hand, but not its finances. The financial situation is precarious. Less than six weeks ago, there was no way of knowing whether the financial situation would allow the school to continue beyond mid-June. This example shows clearly how difficult it is today for such an endeavor to hold its own in the face of the miserable economic conditions of Central Europe, even when it has proved, beyond all doubt, the spiritual justification for its existence. Every month we experience tremendous anxiety over how to make the Waldorf School economically feasible. Destiny allows us to work, but the Sword of Damocles—financial need—is always hanging over our heads. As a matter of principle, we must continue to work as though the school were an eternal establishment. This requires a very devoted teaching staff, who work with inner intensity, never knowing whether they will still be employed in three months.

In any case, anthroposophic education grew out of the Anthroposophical Society. The least sought after prospers best; in other words, what the gods have given, not what we have made, receives the greatest blessing and good fortune. It is quite possible that the art of education must lie especially close to the hearts of anthroposophists. After all, what is truly the most inwardly beautiful thing in the world? Surely it is a growing, developing human being. To see human beings come from spirit worlds and the physical world through birth; to see what lives in them, what they brought down in definite form to gradually become defined as their features and movements; to see properly the divine forces and manifestations working through the human form into the physical world—all this has something that, in the deepest sense, we might call religious. No wonder, then, that wherever there are efforts toward the purest, truest, and most intimate humanity, and where these exist as the very basis of everything anthroposophic, we can contemplate the mystery of the growing human being with sacred, religious feeling that evokes all the work we are capable of.

Arising from the soul's deepest impulses, this evokes real enthusiasm for the art of education within the anthroposophic movement. We can truly say that the art of education exists in the movement as a creation that can be nurtured only through love, and this is how we nurture it. It is indeed nurtured with the utmost devoted love. Many go so far as to say that the Waldorf school is taken to heart by all who know it, and what thrives there does so in a way that must be viewed as inner necessity.

I would like to mention two facts in this connection. Recently, a conference of the Anthroposophical Society was held in Stuttgart. During that conference, a variety of wishes were presented from very different sides. There were proposals about what might be done in different areas of work. And like today, others in the world are very clever, so of course anthroposophists are clever, too; they frequently take part in the world's clever ways. So it happened that a number of suggestions were stated, and one was particularly interesting. It was a suggestion from students in the top class of the Waldorf school—a real appeal to the Anthroposophical Society. It was signed by all the students of class twelve and went more or less as follows: We are being educated in the Waldorf school in a genuine and human way; we dread having to enter an ordinary university or college. Would it be possible for the Anthroposophical Society to create an anthroposophic university? We would like to enter a university in which our education could be as natural and human as it is in the Waldorf school.

This suggestion presented to the meeting and it stirred the members' idealism. As a result, it was decided to begin an anthroposophic university. A considerable sum of money was collected, but then, because of the inflation that occurred, millions of marks simply melted into pfennigs. Nevertheless there were those who believed it might be possible to do something of the kind before the Anthroposophical Society had become strong enough to form and give out judgments. Well, we might be able to train doctors, theologians, and so on, but what would they be able to do after their training? They would not be recognized. Despite this, what was felt by these childlike hearts provides an interesting testimony to the inner necessity of such education. It was certainly not unnatural that such a suggestion was presented.

To continue the story, when our students entered the top class for the first time, we had to do something. We had been able to focus on giving the children a living culture, but now they would have to find a way into the dead culture essential to a college entrance exam. We had to schedule the top class so that the students could pass their test. This cut across our own curriculum, and in our teachers' meetings we found it difficult to limit ourselves to focusing on the examination during the final class year. Nevertheless, this is what we did. I did not find it easy when I visited the class; on the one hand, the students were yawning, because they had to learn what they would have to know for the examination; on the other hand, their teachers often wanted to fit in other subjects that were not required for the examination, but were things that the students wanted to know. They always had to be reminded that they should not say one thing or another at the examination. This was a real difficulty.

And then came the examination. The results were satis-
factory, but in the college of teachers and teachers' meetings, we were completely fed up. We knew that we had
already established the Waldorf school; but now, when
we should crown our work during the last school year,
we could not carry out our intentions and do what the
school requires of us. And so, there and then, despite
everything, we resolved to carry through the curriculum
strictly to the end of the final school year, to the end of the
twelfth class, and moreover to suggest to the parents and
students that we should add another year, so that the
examination could be taken then. The pupils were very
willing to do this, because they saw it as a way to realize
the true intention of the Waldorf school. We experienced
no opposition whatever. There was only one request—
that teachers do the coaching for the exam.

You see how difficult it is in today's "reality" to establish something that originates purely from knowledge of
the human being. Only those who live in a fantasy world
would fail to see that we had to deal with things as they
are and that this leads to great difficulties. On the one
hand, we have the art of education in the anthroposophic
movement, which is loved as a matter of course. On the
other, we have to recognize that the anthroposophic
movement, as it exists in today's society, faces formida-
ble difficulties when it tries to do what it considers an
inner necessity, expecially in the area of education. We
must look reality in the face in a way that is truly alive.

Do not think that I would ever ridicule those who
believe things really aren't so bad or that we make too
much of it all, especially since other schools get along all
right. That's not the point. I know very well how much
effort—and spirit—can be found in today's schools. I

fully recognize this. But unfortunately, people no longer look forward in their thinking. They do not see the threads that connect education, as it has developed in the last few centuries, and what approaches us with the violence of a storm, threatening to ravage and lay our society to waste. Anthroposophy knows the conditions that are essential to developing culture in the future; this alone compels us to develop the methods you find in our education. Our concern is to provide humanity with the possibility of progress and save it from regressing.

On the one hand, I have described how the art of education stands within the anthroposophical movement, but because this art of education is centered in the anthroposophic movement, the movement is itself faced with great difficulties in the public life of today.

So, with an ever increasing group of people coming together, as it happens, and wanting to hear what anthroposophy has to say on the subject of education, we are thankful to the genius of our time that we are able speak about what lies so close to our hearts. In this particular course of lectures, I was able to give a only stimulus and make certain suggestions. But when it comes right down to it, we really haven't accomplished all that much. Our anthroposophic education is based on the actual practice of teaching. It lives only when it is done, because its purpose is nothing more nor less than life itself. In fact, it cannot really be described at all, but must be experienced. This is why, when we try to stimulate interest in what must enter life, we must use of every possible art of speech to show how those who practice the anthroposophic art of education strive to work from the fullness of life. Perhaps I have succeeded only poorly in this course, but I tried. And so you see how our education has grown out of anthroposophy in accordance with destiny.

Many people still live with anthroposophy and want it only as a worldview for heart and soul, and they look with suspicion at anthroposophy when it broadens its area of activity to include art, medicine, education, and so on. But it cannot do otherwise, since anthroposophy requires life. It must work out of life, and it must work into life. Perhaps these lectures on the art of education have succeeded, to some extent, in showing that anthroposophy is in no way sectarian or woven from fantasy, but intended to face the world with the cool reason of mathematics—although, as soon as we enter the spiritual, mathematical coolness engenders enthusiasm, since the word *enthusiasm* itself is connected with spirit, and we cannot help becoming enthusiastic, even if we are cool in the mathematical sense, when we speak and act out of the spirit. Even if anthroposophy is still seen today as an absurd fantasy, it will gradually dawn on people that it is based on absolutely concrete foundations, and that it strives in the widest sense to embody and practice life. And maybe this can be demonstrated best of all today in the area of education.

If I have been able to give some of you a few stimulating ideas, then I am satisfied. Our work together will be best served if those who have been stirred and stimulated a little can, through common effort, find a way to continue in life what these lectures were intended to inspire.

THE FOUNDATIONS
OF WALDORF EDUCATION

THE FIRST FREE WALDORF SCHOOL opened in Stuttgart, Germany, in September 1919, under the auspices of Emil Molt, director of the Waldorf Astoria Cigarette Company and a student of Rudolf Steiner's spiritual science, particularly of Steiner's call for social renewal.

It was only the previous year—amid the social chaos following the end of World War I—that Emil Molt, responding to Steiner's prognosis that truly human change would not be possible unless a sufficient number of people received an education that developed the whole human being, decided to create a school for his workers' children. Conversations with the minister of education and with Rudolf Steiner, in early 1919, then led rapidly to the forming of the first school.

Since that time, more than six hundred schools have opened around the globe—from Italy, France, Portugal, Spain, Holland, Belgium, Britain, Norway, Finland, and Sweden to Russia, Georgia, Poland, Hungary, Romania, Israel, South Africa, Australia, Brazil, Chile, Peru, Argentina, Japan, and others—making the Waldorf school movement the largest independent school movement in the world. The United States, Canada, and Mexico alone now have more than 120 schools.

Although each Waldorf school is independent, and although there is a healthy oral tradition going back to the first Waldorf teachers and to Steiner himself, as well as a growing body of secondary literature, the true foundations of the Waldorf method and spirit remain the many lectures that Rudolf Steiner gave on the subject. For five years (1919–1924), Steiner, while simultaneously working on many other fronts, tirelessly dedicated himself to the dissemination of the idea of Waldorf education. He gave manifold lectures to teachers, parents, the general public, and even the children themselves. New schools were established, and the movement grew.

RUDOLF STEINER'S WORKS ON EDUCATION

I. *Allgemeine Menschenkunde als Grundlage der Pädagogik: Pädagogischer Grundkurs*, 14 lectures, Stuttgart, 1919 (GA 293). Previously *Study of Man*. **The Foundations of Human Experience** (Anthroposophic Press, 1996).

II. *Erziehungskunst Methodische-Didaktisches*, 14 lectures, Stuttgart, 1919 (GA 294). **Practical Advice to Teachers** (Anthroposophic Press, 2000).

III. *Erziehungskunst*, 15 discussions, Stuttgart, 1919 (GA 295). **Discussions with Teachers** (Anthroposophic Press, 1997).

IV. *Die Erziehungsfrage als soziale Frage*, 6 lectures, Dornach, 1919 (GA 296). Previously *Education as a Social Problem*. **Education as a Force for Social Change** (Anthroposophic Press, 1997).

V. *Die Waldorf Schule und ihr Geist*, 6 lectures, Stuttgart and Basel, 1919 (GA 297). **The Spirit of the Waldorf School** (Anthroposophic Press, 1995).

VI. *Rudolf Steiner in der Waldorfschule, Vorträge und Ansprachen*, 24 lectures and conversations and one essay, Stuttgart, 1919–1924 (GA 298). **Rudolf Steiner in the Waldorf School: Lectures and Conversations** (Anthroposophic Press, 1996).

VII. *Geisteswissenschaftliche Sprachbetrachtungen*, 6 lectures, Stuttgart, 1919 (GA 299). **The Genius of Language** (Anthroposophic Press, 1995).

VIII. *Konferenzen mit den Lehrern der Freien Waldorfschule 1919–1924*, 3 volumes (GA 300a–c). **Faculty Meetings with Rudolf Steiner**, 2 volumes (Anthroposophic Press, 1998).

IX. *Die Erneuerung der pädagogisch-didaktischen Kunst durch Geisteswissenschaft*, 14 lectures, Basel, 1920 (GA 301). **The Renewal of Education** (Anthroposophic Press, 2001).

X. *Menschenerkenntnis und Unterrichtsgestaltung*, 8 lectures, Stuttgart, 1921 (GA 302). Previously *The Supplementary Course: Upper School* and *Waldorf Education for Adolescence*. **Education for Adolescents** (Anthroposophic Press, 1996).

XI. *Erziehung und Unterricht aus Menschenerkenntnis*, 9 lectures, Stuttgart, 1920, 1922, 1923 (GA 302a). The first four lectures are in *Balance in Teaching* (Mercury Press, 1982); last three lectures in *Deeper Insights into Education* (Anthroposophic Press, 1988).

XII. *Die gesunde Entwicklung des Menschenwesens*, 16 lectures, Dornach, 1921–22 (GA 303). **Soul Economy: Body, Soul, and Spirit in Waldorf Education** (Anthroposophic Press, 2003).

XIII. *Erziehungs- und Unterrichtsmethoden auf anthroposophischer Grundlage*, 9 public lectures, various cities, 1921–22 (GA 304). **Waldorf Education and Anthroposophy 1** (Anthroposophic Press, 1995).

XIV. *Anthroposophische Menschenkunde und Pädagogik*, 9 public lectures, various cities, 1923–24 (GA 304a). **Waldorf Education and Anthroposophy 2** (Anthroposophic Press, 1996).

XV. *Die geistig-seelischen Grundkräfte der Erziehungskunst,* 12 Lectures, 1 special lecture, Oxford, 1922 (GA 305). *The Spiritual Ground of Education* (Anthroposophic Press, 2004).

XVI. *Die pädagogische Praxis vom Gesichtspunkte geisteswissenschaftlicher Menschenerkenntnis,* 8 lectures, Dornach, 1923 (GA 306). *The Child's Changing Consciousness as the Basis of Pedagogical Practice* (Anthroposophic Press, 1996).

XVII. *Gegenwärtiges Geistesleben und Erziehung,* 14 lectures, Ilkeley, 1923 (GA 307). *A Modern Art of Education* (Anthroposophic Press, 2004) and *Education and Modern Spiritual Life* (Garber Publications, 1989).

XVIII. *Die Methodik des Lehrens und die Lebensbedingungen des Erziehens,* 5 lectures, Stuttgart, 1924 (GA 308). *The Essentials of Education* (Anthroposophic Press, 1997).

XIX. *Anthroposophische Pädagogik und ihre Voraussetzungen,* 5 lectures, Bern, 1924 (GA 309). *The Roots of Education* (Anthroposophic Press, 1997).

XX. *Der pädagogische Wert der Menschenerkenntnis und der Kulturwert der Pädagogik,* 10 public lectures, Arnheim, 1924 (GA 310). *Human Values in Education* (Anthroposophic Press, 2004).

XXI. *Die Kunst des Erziehens aus dem Erfassen der Menschenwesenheit,* 7 lectures, Torquay, 1924 (GA 311). *The Kingdom of Childhood* (Anthroposophic Press, 1995).

XXII. *Geisteswissenschaftliche Impulse zur Entwicklung der Physik. Erster naturwissenschaftliche Kurs: Licht, Farbe, Ton—Masse, Elektrizität, Magnetismus,* 10 lectures, Stuttgart, 1919–20 (GA 320). *The Light Course* (Anthroposophic Press, 2001).

XXIII. *Geisteswissenschaftliche Impulse zur Entwicklung der Physik. Zweiter naturwissenschaftliche Kurs: die Wärme auf der Grenze positiver und negativer Materialität,* 14 lectures, Stuttgart, 1920 (GA 321). *The Warmth Course* (Mercury Press, 1988).

XXIV. *Das Verhältnis der verschiedenen naturwissenschaftlichen Gebiete zur Astronomie. Dritter naturwissenschaftliche Kurs: Himmelskunde in Beziehung zum Menschen und zur Menschenkunde,* 18 lectures, Stuttgart, 1921 (GA 323). In an unpublished manuscript: **"The Relation of the Diverse Branches of Natural Science to Astronomy."**

XXV. *The Education of the Child and Early Lectures on Education* (a collection; Anthroposophic Press, 1996).

XXVI. Miscellaneous.

Intuitive Thinking As a Spiritual Path: A Philosophy of Freedom, Great Barrington, MA: Anthroposophic Press, 1995. Rudolf Steiner lays out the prerequisites for a path of "living" thinking as well as the epistemological foundations for his spiritual scientific observation. This work has also been titled *The Philosophy of Freedom* and *The Philosophy of Spiritual Activity*.

How To Know Higher Worlds: A Modern Path of Initiation, Great Barrington, MA: Anthroposophic Press, 1994. This is Rudolf Steiner's classic account of the modern path of initiation. He gives precise instructions for spiritual practice and descriptions of its results.

Theosophy: An Introduction to the Spiritual Processes in Human Life and in the Cosmos, Great Barrington, MA: Anthroposophic Press, 1994. Steiner presents a comprehensive picture of human nature, beginning with the physical body, moving up through the soul to our spiritual being, with an overview of the laws of reincarnation and the working of karma. He describes a path of knowledge by which we can begin to understand the various ways we live in the worlds of body, soul, and spirit.

An Outline of Esoteric Science, Great Barrington, MA: Anthroposophic Press, 1998. Originally intended to be a continuation of *Theosophy*, this work deals with the nature and evolution of humanity and the cosmos. It also extends and deepens much of what Steiner describes in *Theosophy*. It describes the path of knowledge, including the "Rose Cross meditation," complementing the descriptions in *Theosophy* and *How to Know Higher Worlds*.

A Way of Self-Knowledge, Great Barrington, MA: Anthroposophic Press, 1999. This volume begins with "The Threshold of the Spiritual World," a series of short, aphoristic descriptions of the world and human nature as seen with spiritual vision beyond the boundary between the sensory and spiritual realms. It is intended to present a few descriptions of certain spiritual experiences. From this perspective, these descriptions as well as those in "A Way of Self-Knowledge" should be considered supplementary to the other basic books; nevertheless, these descriptions stand on their own. The eight "meditations" in part two, "A Way of Self-Knowledge," unfolds in the reader and reveal the hidden inner forces that can be awakened in every soul.

INDEX

DURING THE LAST TWO DECADES of the nineteenth century the Austrian-born Rudolf Steiner (1861–1925) became a respected and well-published scientific, literary, and philosophical scholar, particularly known for his work on Goethe's scientific writings. After the turn of the century, he began to develop his earlier philosophical principles into a methodical approach to the research of psychological and spiritual phenomena.

His multifaceted genius led to innovative and holistic approaches in medicine, science, education (Waldorf schools), special education, philosophy, religion, agriculture (biodynamic farming), architecture, drama, movement (eurythmy), speech, and other fields. In 1924 he founded the General Anthroposophical Society, which has branches throughout the world.

Please remember that this is a library book,
and that it belongs only temporarily to each
person who uses it. Be considerate. Do
not write in this, or any, library book.

Printed in the United States
37033LVS00003B/236